conflicted

Pulling Back the Curtain on Public Education

John Stamper

First printing: February 2023

ISBN: 978-1-68344-324-7
ISBN: 978-1-61458-829-0 (digital)
Library of Congress Control Number: 2022951051

Cover by Diana Bogardus

Unless otherwise noted, Scripture quotations are from the King James Version (KJV) of the Bible.

Scripture noted NKJV is from the New King James Version. Copyright © 1982 by Thomas Nelson, Inc. Used by permission. All rights reserved.

Scripture noted ESV is from the English Standard Version®, copyright © 2001 by Crossway, a publishing ministry of Good News Publishers. Used by permission. All rights reserved.

Scripture noted NIV is from the New International Version®, NIV®. Copyright © 1973, 1978, 1984, 2011 by Biblica, Inc.™ Used by permission of Zondervan. All rights reserved worldwide.

Please consider requesting that a copy of this volume be purchased by your local library system.

Printed in the United States of America

Please visit our website for other great titles:
www.masterbooks.com

For information regarding promotional opportunities,
please contact the publicity department at pr@nlpg.com.

Master Books®
A Division of New Leaf Publishing Group
www.masterbooks.com

DEDICATION

To my wife, Jenna, for her love and support.

To my parents — my first teachers — for their continued love and guidance.

Table of Contents

Foreword

In 1990, a husband and wife — both barely 30 years old — made the incredibly difficult decision to pull their four young children out of public school and to teach them at home. With only high school educations, and four rambunctious children under the age of 12 (three boys and a girl), this was an intimidating decision, but one they knew they had to make because they feared for their children's future. They saw where things were going: more and more of the biblical Christian values they wanted instilled in their children were being taught less and less, in favor of secularism, Marxism, and politics. That young set of parents was my mom and dad.

Over 30 years later, in 2021, I made the same decision — to leave public schools — but this time as a teacher. The example set by my parents and the Christian values I learned while home-schooling prepared me to face my own conflict of conscience. My hope is that this book will be a source of encouragement for parents of school-aged children as they face their own conflicts at school.

The Stamper family, 1991: (front, left to right) Phyllis, John, Bobby, Bob, (back) Kelly, Jimmy

Section One:
Beginning at Home

"Whatsoever ye do, do it heartily, as to the Lord, and not unto men; knowing that of the Lord ye shall receive the reward of the inheritance: for ye serve the Lord Christ." — Colossians 3:23–24

1

It's Time to Leave
Public Schools

Public schools are proudly promoting ideologies that are racist, prejudiced, discriminatory, and destructive to our society — all in the name of equity and equality. These ideologies are often kept behind the curtain and snuck in through mandatory staff trainings — where parents and community members cannot see them. The teachers are trained first, then teachers train the students — it's as simple as that. But where are teachers getting these materials and who is pulling the ideological strings? We will discuss this more throughout the book.

America is in a spiritual battle, and public schools have been ground zero for several decades. America's long-held belief in God has been supplanted by the atheist ideologies of Marxism and communism; Critical Race Theory and Gender Theory are two of the byproducts. Not only are these ideologies becoming more common, but they are being embraced, promoted, taught, and defended in public schools and universities. Public schools are a battlefield, and children are on the front lines going up against trained adults in positions of influence and authority — backed by teachers unions and government bodies like the Department of Education. For Christian parents, if you haven't already decided to leave the public schools, you and your children are certain to be faced with a major conflict in values.

> "There is a way that seems right to a man, but its end is the way to death." — Proverbs 14:12; ESV

"There is a way that seems right to a man, but its end is the way to death." — Proverbs 14:12; ESV

As that Proverbs verse rightly points out, two paths are laid out before us — both as individuals and as a nation: 1) we can go our own way, or 2) we can go the way of God. America has turned its back on God, and biblical values can scarcely be found outside of church walls, or sometimes even within church walls. There's perhaps no better example of this than our public school system, which has removed any semblance of biblical morality, is sowing confusion and racial division among students, and has undermined the role of parents, labeling some who dare to speak up as domestic terrorists.

The school closures and virtual classrooms that began in early 2020 with the onset of Covid presented a rare opportunity for the indoctrination process to be streamlined. Teachers could share any image, graph, or document they wanted on screen and take it down in an instant. That means nothing goes home — things can be done in secret, behind the curtain. Parents are never part of the equation.

School Board

▼

Mandatory Trainings

▼

Teachers

▼

Students

Parents may hear about fiery school board meetings or law-suits in the news and on social media, where the topics of CRT and Gender Theory are hot, but many school corpo-rations and districts deny that they are being taught in their schools. Proponents of these ideologies often point to the lack of physical evidence — in essence saying, "Prove it!" That's the tricky part. In many cases, it's difficult to prove that public schools really are teaching Critical Race Theory and Gender Theory, because most schools aren't passing out textbooks and assigning homework on the topics; some absolutely are, but in general it's not the type of information that gets printed out and sent home for parents to see on a regular basis, let alone approve. Often times, as I will discuss later in this book, parents don't know these ideologies are being taught in school until their child comes home with a new pronoun or member-ship to a new, secret club at school.

The indoctrination process became paperless and even more streamlined during the Covid outbreak when school closures and virtual classrooms became the norm — a practice that is still being used by schools around the country. I'll dis-cuss examples of materials that I received as a teacher in man-datory staff trainings and which I was encouraged to share with my students. Teachers could simply show these materials on the screen during virtual classes and take them down in an instant with no physical proof for parents to see. This makes it difficult for parents to see what's going on in school.

The political propaganda I encountered in my teaching for Chicago Public Schools was shocking and I couldn't, in good conscience, go along with what the school system was promulgating. In my last year of teaching for a public school (2020–2021), I experienced the following:

1. Marxist, socialist, and communist ideologies being taught and promoted to students grades K-8

2. Critical Race Theory being used to teach that skin color, gender, sexual orientation, and income level are the most important things about a person

3. Gender Theory, gender dysphoria, and homosexuality being promoted to school-age children as early as kindergarten

4. Society being divided into two groups: oppressors and victims

5. Parents being removed from the education process and intentionally kept in the dark about the most intimate details of their child's life

6. The political-leftist, extremist agenda being instituted as truth — not as one of several competing viewpoints

7. A school board that refused to investigate instances of racial and religious prejudice occurring in their schools

Schools can implement an ideology in a quiet and discreet manner. This can be done through curriculum adoption, mandatory staff trainings, or regular staff meetings — curriculum adoption is the least discreet option, because it provides hard-evidence. Curriculum adoption is when the actual textbooks, workbooks, and programs that kids will be learning from are chosen, so parents would eventually see this stuff (you'd hope). This is usually done every year depending on which textbooks or programs are being pushed. For example, if Common Core is being taught in your school, it's because your teachers, principals, or school board members adopted that curriculum. Critical Race Theory and Gender Theory, which are founded on Marxist and communist ideals, have already taken root in American schools. Not in some other state, not in some other city, not in the future, but right now.

I know that "destructive ideologies" sounds a bit extreme, but that's why I think these ideologies have been able to creep into our public schools over the years — because it's simply hard to believe that something like communism could "take over America." How would schools even get away with something like this?! It happens by keeping the curtain closed to unsuspecting parents and using mandatory staff trainings to implement Critical Race Theory and Gender Theory. "We cannot continue to send our children to Caesar for their education and be surprised when they come home as Romans."[1] It happens because schools have control of kids (yes, control is the right word) for 8 hours a day, 5 days a week, 180 days a year.

I've seen many fads come and go in my 13 years of teaching in public and private schools. For example, I experienced the controversial implementation of Common Core and I've been through numerous math trainings, science trainings, social-emotional trainings, and reading trainings — too many to remember. I've seen them come, and I've seen them go. It seems like the more programs that schools try to implement, the worse the students perform. America's global education ranking, which we will discuss later, will show this to be true.

The difference now is that teachers and students are being taught to see a person's skin color instead of the person. Students are being taught that their "gender identity" is the most important or interesting thing about them, and that they can change genders at any time. Schools are endorsing ideologies that undermine parents and divide society into two groups: the oppressors and the oppressed.

> Schools are endorsing ideologies that undermine parents and divide society into two groups: the oppressors and the oppressed.

Few schools seem to be presenting traditional math and science programs anymore. Instead, schools are using innocent

1. Bauchman, Voddie T., *Family Driven Faith: Doing What it Takes to Raise Sons and Daughters Who Walk With God* (Wheaton, IL: Crossway Books, 2007).

children as guinea pigs to affirm their own political agendas and ideologies. Schools are teaching that if you're not white then you're a victim of systemic racism, that being white is oppressive, that all men are abusive, that being heterosexual is abusive, America is racist, gender is fluid, and that boys can be girls — to name a few.

My goals are to:

1. Share my personal experiences as a Christian teacher in public schools

2. Connect my experiences with other similar stories from around the country

3. Pull back the curtain on the indoctrination process and show parents how mandatory teacher trainings are used to implement radical ideologies in schools

4. Warn parents about public schools that are promoting Critical Race Theory and Gender Theory

5. Show parents how Marxist, socialist, and communist ideologies are dominating public schools

6. Encourage parents to homeschool their children

My belief is that — if your family can do it — it's time to pull your kids out of public schools and begin homeschooling. My hope is to make parents more aware of the dangerous things going on in public schools today, to encourage parents to keep the faith in your homeschooling journey, or to take that initial leap of faith into your homeschooling journey if you haven't done so yet. For families that cannot homeschool or simply choose not to homeschool, I offer the following suggestions:

• Talk to your children daily about what they're learning at school

- Demand that you be involved in your school's textbook and curriculum adoption process

- Demand opportunities to join your school's regular grade level meetings (elementary schools) and department meetings (middle schools and high schools)

- Demand access to all mandatory staff trainings; the same trainings that the teachers complete

- Demand cameras be installed in every classroom (people watch their dogs on camera through the day, so we should be able to watch our children)

- Participate in local elections (school board, sheriff, mayor, state representatives, etc.)

- Run for school board member positions

- Push to have elected school boards instead of appointed school boards

- Attend school board meetings regularly and schedule time to speak and ask questions

- Communicate with teachers and principals on a regular basis

- Join the PTO and attend meetings

- Monitor daily assignments, field trip details, school speakers, and special school assemblies.

I've found that most parents are shocked when I share my recent experiences in the public school system. We all hear things on the news or on social media about destructive ideologies being pushed on students and people might think, "That stuff only happens in the big cities, it would never happen in *my* school." There are certain ways for public schools to implement destructive ideologies or policies without parental consent or knowledge — it's happened already with Common Core and is currently happening with CRT, Gender Theory, Marxism, socialism, and communism.

To be clear, the problem is the government's overreach into education — not the teachers themselves, but the system that allows and promotes destructive ideologies. There are many great teachers who are wonderful role models, but that's becoming less and less the norm as more and more teachers are taking part in the indoctrination process. Not all schools are the same and some have drawn a line in the sand in terms of protecting children from CRT and Gender Theory. Regardless, parents need to know what's going on in schools today. Why? Because you need to be prepared for the conflict of values that is sure to come if you choose to send your kids to a public school. That's why I'm writing this book.

"Darkness cannot drive out darkness, only light can do that." — Martin Luther King Jr.[2]

Homeschooling isn't just an alternative to public and private schooling. Christians who homeschool are a direct rebuttal to the onslaught of wickedness that's taken over our society. Children whose education is founded on biblical and moral truths are the cultural counterpunch to the woke school systems.

If you're worried about the future and what the world will look like for your children and your children's children, take heart in knowing that by raising your children up in the fear and admonition of the Lord, you're working to spread the Light of Christ, not just in the hearts of your children, but in the hearts of all the people they will meet in their future. This is the good fight.

In all things, it's important to learn from history. Many say that history repeats itself, but I like how my former history professor taught it. He explained that history is not a

---

2. https://www.gardnerkansas.gov/Home/Components/News/ News/684/72?arch=1.

repetitive circle, but it's more like a helix that spirals upward; we may recognize similarities between different points in history, but there is never really a true repetition of history. It is imperative that Americans understand world history, particularly instances when government authorities used the education system to implement their political ideologies, so that we can change course as a nation and avoid the tragedies that took place in the 20th century.

My wife and I traveled to Poland in 2019 and were able to tour Auschwitz; it was one of the most impactful experiences of my life. We saw the train tracks that led the boxcars full of Jewish families to the platform where the selection process occurred — who would go straight to the gas chambers and who would be forced into slave labor and eventual death. We saw the bunk houses, latrines, and prisons. We saw the mountain of shoes that were collected from the victims, so many of whom were children. We saw the ovens where the dead bodies were cremated. But perhaps the most shocking and lasting image was the encased room of human hair. The Nazi soldiers would shave the heads of the prisoners upon arrival and use the human hair as a resource, like fabric. When Auschwitz was liberated in 1945, there were stores of human hair still preserved and now encased at Auschwitz to serve as a reminder of what happened there.

Those horrors were the end results, but how could something like that ever begin in the first place? The education system played a major role.

Adolph Hitler came to power in Germany in 1933. He immediately began to reform the German education system to support the National Socialist party. Hitler's indoctrination process was so successful that in less than a decade of his reign, scores of German children were taken from their parents to form the *Hitler Youth*, serve as Nazi soldiers, and eventually carry out the horrors of the Holocaust during WWII. The Nazi propaganda machine was so powerful that, when the time came, regular German citizens would turn in

Jewish neighbors to the Gestapo. The following statement describes how Germany fell to such a dark state.

> Everything that has been built up over a century of work by the teaching profession is no longer there in essence. . . . They have been willfully destroyed from above. No thought any more of proper working methods in school, or of the freedom of teaching. In their place we have cramming and beating schools, prescribed methods of learning and . . . learning materials. Instead of freedom of learning, we have the most narrow-minded school supervision and spying on teachers and pupils. No free speech is permitted for teachers and pupils, no inner, personal empathy. The whole thing has been taken over by the military spirit.[3]

Below were steps taken to imbed Nazi propaganda into the German education system.

Change the school curriculum
- Inject race into the curriculum; teach that certain races are superior, and some are inferior.[4]

Position individuals within the system to support the agenda
- Hitler appointed Bernhard Rust as Minister of Education whose role was to rid the educational system of Nazi opponents.[5]

Gain student support of political agenda
- Students were taught to stand and raise their hands toward a picture of Hitler on the classroom wall.[6]

---

3. Richard Evans, *The Third Reich in Power* (NY: Penguin Books, 2005), p. 270.
4. Cate Haste, *Nazi Women* (Channel 4 Books, 2001) p. 101.
5. Louis L. Snyder, *Encyclopedia of the Third Reich* (Cody, WY: WordsWorth Publishing, 1998), p. 303.
6. Tomi Ungerer, *Tomi: A Childhood under the Nazis* (Roberts Rinehart Publishers 1998), p. 63.

Replace textbooks
- Old texts were replaced with new texts that supported National Socialism.[7]

Replace teachers
- All Jewish teachers were dismissed from teaching in German schools and universities in 1933. Races were separated into different schools to maintain racial purity.[8]

Train new teachers
- Most teachers were required to complete mandatory trainings which urged support for Hitler and the Nazi regime; teachers were then expected to train their students accordingly.[9]

Undermine the family unit
- Teachers encouraged students to report if their parents were not Nazi supporters, demanding their allegiance to Hitler.[10]

Keep these strategies in mind as you continue to read through this book and as I share my public school experiences. There are chilling similarities between how the ideology of the Nazi educational system and the current American public school system were incorporated.

Education is important, but the *type* of education is more important. Prior to Hitler and the rise of the Nazi party, Germany had the reputation as being one of the most highly-educated societies on the planet — known for its school system, high literacy rates, and esteemed universities. As of 1913, Germany published more books annually than any other country.[11] It did not take long for that to all be torn down.

7. Evans, *The Third Reich in Power*, p. 264.
8. Bernhard Rust, *National Socialist Germany and the Pursuit of Learning* (1936).
9. Snyder, *Encyclopedia of the Third Reich*, p. 79.
10. Michael Burleigh, *The Third Reich: A New History* (2001), p. 236.
11. https://www.intellectualtakeout.org/blog/nazi-germany-was-highly-educated/.

DEFINITIONS

Marxism, socialism, and communism will be discussed throughout this book, as well as their offspring — Critical Race Theory and Gender Theory. Below are reminders of some key characteristics of these systems:

Marxism:
- Social, political, and economic theory that separates people based on class, race, and gender
- Casts one group as the *oppressor* and the other group as the *oppressed*
- The goal is to establish communism
- Atheist

Socialism:
- People do all the work
- Government distributes the goods, services, and money as it sees fit
- Everyone gets equal wealth and provisions (in theory)
- Disincentivizes hard work and creativity; promotes greed, mediocrity, and laziness
- The goal is to establish communism

Communism:
- People do not own land, resources, or businesses
- Often results in forced labor
- Government owns everything and determines who gets what
- Promotes class warfare and creates extreme levels of poverty
- Atheist

Free-Market Capitalism:
- People own land, resources, and businesses (private property)
- Free exchange of goods and services; mutually beneficial
- Government enforces laws and doesn't interfere with the market (ideally)
- Supply and demand drives the economy and promotes competition
- Promotes creativity and growth
- Rewards hard work; allows for unequal levels of wealth

Vladimir Lenin famously stated that, "The goal of socialism is communism."[12] As history proves, governments must use force, fear, coercion, and power to achieve Marxism, socialism, or communism, all of which are ideologies that have been embraced and implemented by the most brutal dictators in human history. They encourage sacrifice of anything to achieve "utopia," which is why such governments of the 20th century were able to perpetrate the most significant mass murders on their own citizens.

Vladimir Lenin famously stated that, "The goal of socialism is communism."

Marxist, socialist, and communist ideologies are entirely evil. Disturbingly, as I will point out, many of these ideological principles are being implemented and glorified in Chicago Public Schools, and schools around the country, through mandatory staff trainings and then through teacher-student interactions.

---

12. https://www.brainyquote.com/quotes/vladimir_lenin_136421.

2

My Personal Testimony

Before we get into the serious issues that families are facing in public schools today, I want to share a bit about myself — my upbringing, my salvation story, and my career as a teacher and coach. I believe it will give context to my story and my point of view.

I was born in 1985, the youngest of four. When I was three years old, my parents moved our family from the Chicago suburbs to small-town Indiana. My siblings and I grew up on 50 acres of farmland and wooded pasture. Both of my parents were new Christians by the time I was born, so I was raised in a Christian home my entire life; that's all I've ever known. For most of my childhood, my parents took us to church on Sunday morning, Sunday night, and to Bible study on Wednesday night. We had regular Bible studies at home or at a family member's house. We even held potluck-sing-a-longs where people from church would come to our house, bring food, bring instruments, and we'd have a praise and worship service right there in our house. Most kids would probably want to go play and let the adults do the adult things, but I actually really enjoyed those nights as a kid and I really long for them now — nothing can replace the Presence of God! I would not describe my parents as religious, rather I would say they loved the Lord and wanted to fellowship with other believers as much as possible — it was always about relationship, not religion.

In my teenage years, I did not have a personal relationship with Christ. My time, energy, thoughts, concerns, and heart were consumed by anything and everything other than God. Concerts, parties, friends, movies, girls, sports — you name it. My parents did a great job teaching us the Word of God, but I had not experienced God personally yet. I knew the stories of the Bible and I knew it was all true. I believed the Bible to be the inspired Word of God ... but I did not *know* Him. I had the head-knowledge, but I did not have the heart-knowledge. My parents had a wonderful, powerful, and miraculous salvation story, but their salvation was not my salvation — that was something I had to receive myself.

I graduated high school in 2003 and went off to college at Indiana University that fall. At the time, IU was ranked the #1 party school in the country (whatever that means) and it lived up to the hype. Having "fun" was the top priority for my friends and me. What I considered to be "fun" at the time was really just a reflection of my sinful lifestyle; it was fun on weekends but miserable, lonely, and unfulfilling during the week. Sometimes God lets us sink so low that we have no place else to look but up. That was the case for me. I had sunken to the lowest point of my life — socially, emotionally, and most importantly, spiritually.

Thank God for godly parents who pray for their children!

In the spring of 2004, during my second semester of college, God began to draw me out of my self-centered world and unto Himself. Over a two or three-week period and through a series of seemingly insignificant, unimportant events, the Holy Spirit got my attention and showed me my true spiritual condition, and I thank God for that.

It wasn't long until I was back visiting the church I'd grown up in and responding to an altar call. I remember, as I knelt to pray the sinner's prayer, that the song "Amazing Love" was being played. I wanted to know Him as well as He knew me and I remember the moment I was saved; it was as if a million pounds was lifted off my shoulders and, even though my eyes were closed, all I could see was light — I was brought from darkness into the glorious light! That was in February of 2004 and I'm still living for the Lord today.

My parents getting saved changed the whole trajectory of my family; it changed our future. If my parents cared nothing for God or the Bible, they would not have made the decision to pull my siblings and me out of public school.

MY TEACHING BACKGROUND

I graduated from Indiana University in 2008 with a Bachelor's in Elementary Education (K–6) and a minor in Special Education (K–12). After graduation, I stayed in my hometown and taught 6th grade, which included the core subjects (Math, Reading, Science, History). In year two, I moved to Knoxville, Tennessee, and became an after-school teacher for a private school. There, I was responsible for the 2nd–5th grade students that were involved in the program — mostly helping with after-school studies. I left Knoxville and returned home to northwest Indiana in 2010, where I began my third year of teaching at a private treatment facility for kids. At the same time I returned to college to add Physical Education and Health & Wellness (K–12) to my teaching degree. The children living at this facility were court-ordered to live there. These youth came from difficult backgrounds and were often predisposed to violence, drug abuse, or expulsions from school. At this treatment facility, I was responsible for teaching boys from age 12 to 17. It was a one-room-schoolhouse environment where I had to meet each student at his individual grade level while still teaching all students as a group. This was the most difficult experience of my life, but also provided me the most freedom I've ever had as a teacher. I was able to craft the curriculum to tailor my students and teach subjects they were interested in. In this way, the one-room-schoolhouse approach, which is like homeschooling, is superior to today's public schools.

In 2011, I left the treatment facility and landed what would become my dream job — teaching Elementary Physical Education. During my nine-year tenure in Munster, Indiana, I earned my Master's in Leadership & Sport Management from Trine University. When schools closed during the 2020 Covid outbreak, I created an educational website that offered online P.E. courses to students that were unexpectedly stuck at home. These online courses have since opened the door to a career in homeschooling, for which I've left my career in public schools.

In addition to my 14 years of teaching, I've also enjoyed 13 years of coaching. I've been a volunteer coach, assistant coach, and head coach in five different sports, ranging from elementary to varsity athletes. I began as a volunteer coach for my old high school baseball team. This initial coaching position opened the door for an assistant position as a high school swim coach as well as an assistant position as an elementary basketball coach. The swim coach position led to me becoming the Pool Director for the entire school corporation. The director position led to my next position as head coach of a tiny high school track and field team, which then led to my position as head coach of a huge high school track and field team. Since childhood, I have consistently found myself in leadership positions, whether it was as a team captain, supervisor, coach, or teacher. In my experience, one opportunity has led to another.

3

The Gideons, Atheists, and Phil Donahue

My parents grew up in the 1960s and 1970s; they got married as teenagers and started having kids right away. In fact, they both dropped out of high school in the 1970s and decided to go to work instead (they both eventually finished high school and my dad went on to earn a college degree). It's hard to imagine in today's world, but back then you didn't need a degree to make a good living. By 1988 and four kids later, my parents decided to move to the country and give us kids a better life, so we moved to Rensselaer, Indiana — a rural farming community. We had plenty of space to run wild and were far away from the hustle and bustle of the city. My siblings were enrolled in the local public schools, but I was a toddler and still too young for school.

At the time, the Rensselaer Central School Corporation held a long-time policy which allowed for various groups in the community to visit their schools and distribute literature — whether it be for Little League, 4-H, Boys Scouts, or Girl Scouts. One such group was the Gideon Society. For anyone who may not know, the Gideons are a group that donates Bibles to schools, hotels — basically anyone that will take them — but they do so free of charge and without coercion. The Gideons had been welcomed to distribute Bibles to fifth grade students since before anyone could remember. Two representatives would visit the school once a year and speak for a couple of minutes. They'd always end their speech by offering free Bibles to any fifth graders who might be interested.

In 1990, a parent of two elementary-aged students filed a complaint against the school corporation, claiming that the school's practice of allowing religious materials to be distributed in school violated the Constitution.[1] The topic of "separation of church and state" was being heavily debated during the late 1980s and early 1990s — if Twitter was a thing back then, #churchandstate would have been a trending topic. The case was heard in District Court, and the initial ruling was in favor of the School Board. However, the case went on to be heard in the Indiana Supreme Court the following year and the district court's decision was reversed in favor of the plaintiff — prohibiting the school from allowing the Gideons to distribute their Bibles.[2]

My parents were disappointed in the court's decision and were concerned for the educational and spiritual well-being of their children. As new Christians, my parents had a strong desire to give us a biblical education and instill Christian values in us. They were barely 30 years old with four kids under the age of 12, and they were faced with the same difficult decision so many families are faced with today — should we pull our kids out of public school or not?

My mom decided to express her concern by writing a letter to the editor of the local newspaper, *The Rensselaer Republican*. Her letter was published and titled, "Absence of Bible leads to moral decay." She wrote about America's godly heritage and

---

1. https://casetext.com/case/berger-v-rensselaer-central-school/.
2. https://casetext.com/case/berger-v-rensselaer-cent-schoolcorp/?sort=relevance&resultsNav=false&q=.

that the Bible was the principal text in America's schools for generations. Since America's beginning, students had been taught the Ten Commandments, to love God, love your neighbor, don't lie, and don't murder. She referenced the correlation of rising

Since America's beginning, students had been taught the Ten Commandments, to love God, love your neighbor, don't lie, and don't murder.

crime rates, divorce rates, anxiety, depression, and suicide in America with the removal of biblical morality in schools. She urged parents and those in authority over our children to pray for wisdom concerning this modern secular trend.

Weeks later, our phone rang, and my mom answered. It was a staff member from the Maury Povich show, inviting her and my dad to be guests on their show. My mom struggled to understand how and why they were calling her until they mentioned her letter to the editor. Somehow, some way, *Associated Press* in New York City picked up my mom's letter to the *Rensselaer Republican* and published it in their newspaper, which is a worldwide publication. She had no idea this had happened! She told them she would have to talk it over with my dad and call them back. A few minutes later, the Phil Donahue show called and offered to fly her and my dad out to New York City to appear on his show and debate America's most well-known atheist, Madalyn Murray O'Hair — founder and president of the American Atheists.

Before you know it, both of my parents — an ironworker and a stay-at-home mom — were being flown out to the Big Apple to debate the most influential atheist in America on national television. Like most talk show guests, my parents sat backstage before the show and before it was time for filming to begin, my dad walked down the hall to use the rest room. It just so happened that as he entered the hallway, so did Madalyn Murray O'Hair. While passing each other, O'Hair asked my dad, "You're from Indiana, aren't you?" My dad, surprised that she even knew him since they had never met before, confirmed that he was indeed from Indiana and O'Hair responded, "Those

Gideons are slime." O'Hair was referring to the Gideons that were distributing Bibles in my small hometown.

My parents were seated in the front row, surrounded by an audience of O'Hair's atheist supporters. Throughout the taping, O'Hair bad-mouthed Christians, claiming that they hated her and that they've contributed very little to society. The filming of the show had almost wrapped up and my parents had still not been called on to speak. It was customary of the Donahue Show to have viewers call in to ask questions or to allow audience members to hold the microphone to ask their questions. With just a few minutes left of filming, Phil Donahue finally introduced my parents, but this time he held the microphone himself. Perhaps he had a feeling that things might get testy between Ms. O'Hair and my parents.

Even though my mom's letter is what sparked this whole journey, it was my dad who did the speaking when addressing O'Hair. This was not something my parents had planned, it just happened that way. I always looked at it as a great example of how a marriage should work — both members have unique talents and gifts but balance each other perfectly.

When the time came to speak, my dad spoke directly to Ms. O'Hair and said, "I'm a Christian and I don't hate you. I love you and Jesus loves you, too." He gave his testimony of how Jesus Christ saved him from drunkenness and a life of sin and mentioned all the good that Christianity has done for the world — churches, schools, hospitals. He mentioned how the phrase "separation of church and state" is not in the Constitution, but it can be found in the governing documents of the USSR. He mentioned that O'Hair's own son, a preacher of the Gospel, had been saved by the blood of Jesus Christ — a fact that O'Hair did not like to be reminded of. Before he knew it, Phil Donahue pulled the microphone away and went to a commercial break. My dad remembers

He mentioned how the phrase "separation of church and state" is not in the Constitution, but it can be found in the governing documents of the USSR.

that during the commercial break, O'Hair shouted obsceni-
ties at him — apparently, she did not like what he had to say.

The show ended without fanfare, no spotlights, no
post-show interviews. In total, my parents were given about
one-minute of camera time — a seemingly small amount of
time, considering all the trouble my parents went through to
get there. However, we cannot underestimate God's ability to
use even a single minute of our time — little is much when
God is in it. Tragically, a few years after the Donahue Show
experience, Madalyn Murray O'Hair was kidnapped and bru-
tally murdered along with one of her sons and a granddaugh-
ter — all were members of the American Atheists.

As the dust settled from my parents' whirlwind talk show
experience, we began our first year of homeschooling in the
early 1990s. My siblings and I spanned four grade levels that
first year: kindergarten, 2nd, 4th, and 6th grade. My dad was
an ironworker and worked mostly in Chicago, a three-hour
round-trip every day, so my mom took on the responsibility
of being our teacher. She was scared and nervous about taking
on the daunting task of homeschooling four kids, but she held
on to the belief that there is nothing too big for God! She and
my dad sought the Lord in prayer, and He promised that He
would help every step of the way. For my parents, the priority was God's Word. They had set their hearts and minds on
following the Lord and that meant raising their kids to have a
biblical worldview.

MY HOMESCHOOLING EXPERIENCE

We spent most of the 1990s homeschooling. This was before
computers were a thing, so we relied on textbooks (what a
concept). My mom said that I was her worst student because
I never wanted to sit still or do my work (maybe that's why
I spent most of my career as a P.E. teacher). Looking back,
I have only the fondest memories of my homeschooling

experience. I appreciate the freedom we had as a family to work at our own pace and on our own schedule. I appreciate the efficiency homeschooling provided and the quality time we enjoyed together as a homeschool family. Most of all, I appreciate the opportunities I had to learn from my parents that God loves us so much that He gave His only Son, Jesus, to save us from our sin and that no matter where we went in life, we would always have the promise of eternal life in Christ Jesus.

My parents held the line and homeschooled their kids for most of the 90's — focusing on biblical principles, work ethic, and academics. We would start school at 8:00 a.m. (just like the public school kids) and we would usually be done by 10:00 a.m., which is about five hours sooner than the local public schools — this shows how much time is wasted in public schools. My parents were very clever in finding ways to keep us busy. We had a big yard and plenty of space growing up, so there was never a shortage of chores to do after school: pulling weeds, picking up sticks, cutting down a tree, chopping wood, raking gravel back into the driveway, mowing grandma's lawn. This went on for years … and years … and years.

After six years of homeschooling, my siblings and I reached middle school and high school and we wanted to play team sports. For years we had all played Little League during the summer months, but the local schools at that time did not permit homeschool kids to join the public-school teams. So, in 1995 my parents made the cautious decision to enroll us back into public school, only this time it would be in a neighboring school system. I know the decision to stop homeschooling was hard for my parents — especially after the physical, emotional, and spiritual battles they went through to begin homeschooling — but they were successful in their quest. They gave my siblings and me a biblical foundation, taught us Christian values, and we all entered the public school system at or above grade level. This is how they prepared us for public school and the rest of our lives. I'll always remember and appreciate the reasons *why* I was homeschooled. As Proverbs 22:6 says, "Train up a child in the way he should go: and when he is old, he will not depart from it."

"Train up a child in the way he should go: and when he is old, he will not depart from it."
Proverbs 22:6

I don't fully understand all the reasons why God led my parents down this path, but I am absolutely convinced that He orchestrated every one of these events. One tangible result from the *Associated Press/Donahue Show* experience was that people from all over the country began to write letters to my parents, thanking them for taking a biblical stand and defending Christian values. I often think that maybe there was an atheist somewhere in America watching the show in support of Madeline Murray O'Hair and they heard my dad say Jesus loves them. Perhaps they reconsidered their ways and even gave their life to Christ. Or maybe there was another young family facing a similar public school crisis and perhaps my mom's letter encouraged them to homeschool. At the very least, my parents gave my siblings and me an example to follow. Their experience impressed upon us just how important the Word of God is and the absolute dependence we must have on Him. I sometimes wonder how different things would have been for my siblings and me if my parents left us in public school, never wrote a letter, never homeschooled us, never took a stand.

The decision to homeschool your children can be scary and intimidating; it was no different for my parents when they homeschooled us, and it was no different for me when I decided to leave my career as a public school teacher. At the time, neither of my parents had graduated high school and they were concerned about their ability to homeschool their children. As my parents went to God in prayer, He would remind them of how He took my mom's letter and turned it into a nationally televised mini-sermon — something only God can do. God assured them that if they would simply be obedient to His leading and guiding, He would take care of the rest. You may be stuck in a valley of decision, not sure if you should stick it out with the public schools or try homeschooling. Know that you're not alone and that families all over America are facing the same decision.

If you're a parent facing a conflict and you feel you're in a spiritual battle, know that your children are watching and what you do will stick with them. I encourage you to prayerfully make your decisions and obey God's Word; you will set a godly example for your children to follow. For me, I'll always remember why I was homeschooled. It's not *that* I was homeschooled, it's *why* I was homeschooled that matters most.

The difference maker for my parents was that — before they even considered homeschooling — they were in daily fellowship with God through prayer and Bible study. Imperfect as my parents were (as we all are) — they knew how to pray. They knew how to reach God. They knew His Word and they were faithful to it. God honors faith that is placed in His Son Jesus and what He did on the Cross. My dad recalls that as he was reading the Bible and praying

> *The difference maker for my parents was that — before they even considered homeschooling — they were in daily fellowship with God through prayer and Bible study.*

the night before their appearance on the Phil Donahue show, the Holy Spirit led him to an encouraging scripture from Acts 18:9-10: "Be not afraid, but speak, and hold not thy peace: For I am with thee, and no man shall set on thee to hurt thee: for I have much people in this city." God provided for my parents during their time of difficulty, and He met every one of their needs. I don't remember many assignments I completed during my years of homeschooling and I don't remember many school projects. I do remember the reasons *why* I was homeschooled. My parents, through their actions, taught my siblings and me that the Word of God is to be the top priority in our lives. It is to reign supreme over our lives. If you get the Bible wrong, it doesn't matter what else you may get right. My encouragement to you is to seek the Lord and hear from Him for yourself.

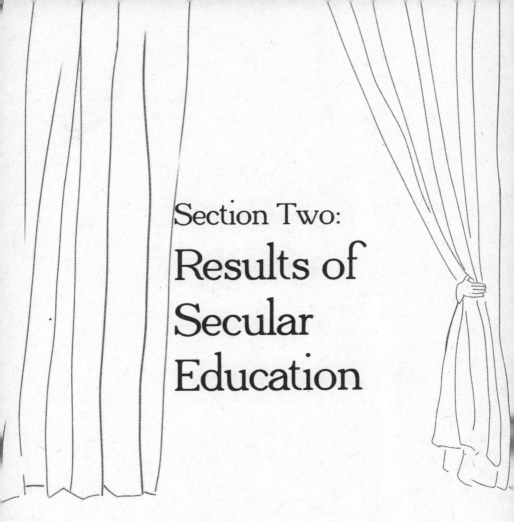

Section Two:
Results of Secular Education

"The whole head is sick, and the whole heart faint."
— Isaiah 1:5

4

My Personal Experience in Mandatory Staff Trainings in Chicago Public Schools

Shortly after I married my wife and moved to Chicago, I started looking for teaching jobs in the city (since my position at the time was in Indiana, and it was a long commute every day). After applying to several private schools, Christian schools, and public schools in Chicago, I was hired to teach P.E. to K–8th grade students at a reputable public school in the heart of the city and I held that position with Chicago Public Schools for just one year.

I started in August of 2020, during the first full school year of the Covid pandemic; all CPS schools began the school year totally remote. Fortunately, I was somewhat prepared for the virtual learning because I had just launched my own set of online P.E. courses that spring, in addition to teaching my students remotely during that spring. The year began as typical as possible, given everyone was remote and I had met only a few of my new colleagues in person and none of my students. Like every other year at every other school, I was required to complete mandatory staff training throughout the school year, which is common practice for businesses and schools around the country. Teachers are usually required to complete two or three different trainings each school year, and those trainings made sense — for example, sexual harassment, disease protocol, different teaching methodologies or ideas, and the like. However, the staff trainings I was required to complete in CPS were different than any training I'd ever taken before.

In the fall of 2020, right around Thanksgiving and Christmas, CPS staff members were required to complete a round of mandatory trainings. There were about a dozen short videos in this particular training bundle, most of which are available to the public and can be found on YouTube. The images, graphs, videos, and narrations that were in this training bundle were shocking to me, openly presenting Marxist theories and other divisive philosophies as factually true (not a theory, matter of opinion, or up for interpretation). At the time, Chicago Public Schools employed over 20,000 teachers and taught nearly 350,000 students. Every single teacher was mandated to take these trainings, which meant that every single teacher was presented with Critical Race Theory and Gender Theory as being true, not as one or two theories among several.

Given that 2020–2021 was an unprecedented school year, I expected that the mandatory trainings would revolve around one (or some) of the several issues that were implicated by the pandemic — for example, a little extra training on how to teach remotely, or preventing the spread of diseases, or even how to ensure that students with disabilities who were used to individual aid in the classroom would not be lost in the remote world. That was not the case. In the middle of the Covid pandemic, everyone's first year of remote learning, social distancing, and mask-wearing — Chicago Public Schools decided to train its staff members on topics such as:

- "How to support transgender, non-binary, and gender-nonconforming students"
- "Pronouns"
- "What does transgender mean"
- "Intersectionality"

At best, these training topics were irrelevant and out of place; at worst, they were divisive, prejudiced, biased, racist, and discriminatory toward teachers and students.

For the first time in my life, I was teaching Physical Education over a computer to hundreds of K–8th grade students, and instead of being provided with the resources I needed to do my job, the school board decided to train all teachers on far left, political ideologies — and I was expected to integrate these theories into my class. This was baffling to me; my job was to teach students how to throw, catch, kick, play sports, and stay fit — not affirm them if they wanted to change genders, act as if their skin color determines their life, apologize for being a man, or for being white.

According to the Chicago Public School Board, who is responsible for selecting training materials for its teachers, I was indeed supposed to talk about white privilege, male privilege, intersectionality, and what it means to be transgender in my elementary P.E. classes; the training videos explicitly called for it. The whole point of these mandatory teacher trainings was for teachers to take this information into their classrooms and teach it to their students. For a long time, this is what parents were not seeing. For months and years even, many skeptics around the country said that no schools were teaching CRT and Gender Theory — but they made those claims because it was all hidden and kept only between the staff and the students. All done behind the proverbial curtain and under the parental radar.

I'm going to provide examples that were taken directly from these trainings — things I experienced first-hand — and explain the connection between these trainings and Marxist, socialist, and communist ideologies. These damaging, pseudo-intellectual, and divisive trainings are exactly why I resigned from my position at CPS and exactly why parents should pull their kids out of school corporations like this. To be clear, Marxism is atheistic. So is socialism and so is communism. If you're a believer, you can be sure that the public school system is at enmity with the Word of God. No ifs, ands, or buts about it.

I was a teacher in this kind of environment, and I was made to feel like an enemy. I fit the description of the enemy (according to my employer) because I'm a white male, straight, in my thirties, a Christian, non-disabled, English speaking, and identify with my sex at birth. These things, according to Chicago Public Schools, make me privileged, oppressive, and abusive — as demonstrated in the training materials mentioned in this chapter. Not only that, but this propaganda declares anyone that is different from me as marginalized, as a victim, up against it, disadvantaged, less than, poor, abused, and manipulated. These ideologies were being applied in the classrooms and presented to teachers as truth, not theory. That's what was happening in the Chicago Public Schools and in many public schools around the country, as you will see in this chapter.

⁂

INTERSECTING IDENTITIES

The following information is based on a training video I was required to view in 2020 while teaching for CPS. There was a graphic that was created by the California Partnership to End Domestic Violence, and the video topic was on "Intersectionality," and was not presented as theory, but as fact.[1] The graphic placed every individual, teacher, student, staff member, and parent into one of two groups: "Privileged" or "Marginalized." The narrator of the video described the graphic in this way:

---

1. https://www.youtube.com/watch?v=alukdZlrDp4).

Here you will find a graphic representation of the various ways in which individuals who hold privilege over another may use tactics of abuse to further oppress an individual or group of individuals.

Look again at the language used in this training video:

… individuals who hold privilege over another may use tactics of abuse to further oppress an individual or group of individuals.

Here is a list of the nine "privileged" groups and nine "marginalized" groups as presented in the video:

Privileged Groups	Marginalized Groups
1. White People	1. People of Color
2. Boys/Men	2. Girls/Women
3. Cisgender People	3. Transgender, Queer, Gender Non-conforming
4. Wealthy, Homeowners, Upper/Middle Class	4. Financially Poor, Working Class
5. Heterosexual/Straight	5. LGBTQ+
6. Adults (18–65)	6. Children, Youth, Older Adults
7. Native English Speakers	7. Non-Native English Speakers
8. Christians	8. Non-Christians
9. People without Disabilities	9. People with Disabilities

So, what is being said here? What exactly is the school system trying to impose on its teachers and students through this information? Applying simple logic and objectivity to this graphic, Chicago Public Schools hold the following opinions of their own staff, students, and parents:

- If you're white, then you're abusive and manipulative.
- If you're not white, then you're a victim of both abuse and manipulation.
- If you're a boy, then you're abusive and a threat.
- If you're a girl, then you're both a victim of abuse and in danger.
- If you're a Christian, then you're abusive.

- If you're not a Christian, then you're a victim of abuse.
- If you're straight, then you're abusive and you use children.
- If you're homosexual, then you're a victim of abuse.

This is a clear example of Critical Race Theory being taught in public schools. This is Marxism 101. A key feature of Marxism is to pit individuals against each other as the "oppressor" on one side versus the "oppressed" on the other side. Parents, how would you feel about this

A key feature of Marxism is to pit individuals against each other as the "oppressor" on one side versus the "oppressed" on the other side.

being taught to your children at school, and without your knowledge or consent? In this ideology, everything in life is determined by your immutable characteristics — skin color, sex, age, sexual orientation, language, and physical abilities. Nothing is said of your *actual* behaviors. The way you *actually* treat people is never considered. The *actual* content of one's character is not mentioned. What type of environment is created when schools teach this to their staff and students? How could such an environment be anything other than divisive, angry, and volatile?

There are 17 different instances of racism, prejudice, and discrimination in this one graphic, which has been adopted and promoted by Chicago Public Schools. In this graphic, the term "privilege" is neither a positive term nor one of unity, rather it's a divisive term and a way to dehumanize other people. Being labeled as "privileged" is an indictment and a reason to be discredited as an individual or group of individuals. According to the graphic, being labeled as "privileged" means you are emotionally and economically abusive, threatening, intimidating, and manipulative of systems. The whole point is to identify the "privileged" groups and their "oppressive" behaviors in order to blame and delegitimize them.

The use of the term "marginalized" is equally prejudiced, even though it is postured as offering sympathy to a person or group of people. The point is that this type of training promotes and even instructs teachers (and, by proxy, students) to make judgments about people based solely on their skin color, sex, or religion — it teaches and promotes prejudice, even if the goal is to garner sympathy. It is wrong to draw conclusions about someone's life, character, behavior, abilities, worldview, based solely on their skin color, age, gender, or other immutable characteristics — period. Racism, prejudice, bias, and discrimination are taking place on a massive scale and being forced on the most vulnerable and impressionable group of our society — children. The categorization and separation of people based on race, gender, class, orientation, religion — which is demonstrated in these trainings — are divisive, completely secular, and are hallmarks of Marxism. These ideals cause division, not unity. They cause destruction, not "healing" — a term that is so commonly used by those promulgating destructive ideologies. They stoke hatred toward God and one another, not love.

In another training video, the narrator states that misgendering a transgender person is an act of oppression. This is yet another example of divisive, Marxist ideologies being promulgated to teachers in the hopes that it flows down to the children. In the training video, the narrator goes on to say:

> "Wealthy people can be oppressive of low-income people by hoarding wealth and not engaging in mutual aid that enables the redistribution of wealth and resources."

Again, consider the language used:

> "… hoarding wealth…redistribution of wealth…."

Applying simple logic and objectivity only leads to the following conclusions:

- Owning a home and building wealth are oppressive acts.
- Saving money that you've earned is "hoarding" and economically abusive.
- Redistribution of wealth (also known as socialism) is the right thing to do.

Whatever happened to working hard, saving money, creating a home and life for you and your family, and doing unto others as you'd have them do unto you? Apparently, according to our school system, we must toss out the American Dream and replace it with socialism — and those who do not agree with that sentiment are oppressive. This has nothing to do with charity or caring for the less fortunate. The Church should be the first to participate in helping those in need, but not because of coercion, but out of love and service to the Lord.

According to the "Intersecting Identities" graphic below, wherever two "privileged groups" meet, there is an "Intersecting Identity" and a corresponding act of oppression. There are eight such identities/acts of oppression:

Intersecting Identities	Oppressive Actions
White People + Boys/Men	Emotional Abuse toward People of Color and Girls/Women
Boys/Men + Cisgender People	Intimidation and Threats toward Girls/Women and Transgender, Queer, Gender Non-Conforming individuals
Wealthy, Homeowners, Upper/Middle Class + Heterosexual/Straight	Economic Abuse toward Financially Poor, Working Class and LGBTQ+ individuals
Heterosexual/Straight + Adults (18–65)	Using Children
Adults (18–65) + Native English Speakers	Blaming and Minimizing Children, Youth, Older Adults, and Non-Native English Speakers

Christians + Native English Speakers	Using Status over Non-Christians and Non-Native English Speakers
Christians + People without Disabilities	Emotional Abuse toward Non-Christians and People with Disabilities
White People + People without Disabilities	Using Knowledge of Systems against People of Color and People with Disabilities

Applying logic and objectivity, one can only draw the following conclusions:

- Stating that white men are abusers (merely just because they are (i) white and (ii) men) promotes certain skin colors over others and one gender over another. That's discrimination. It's a predetermined, harmful, and hateful generalization of people based on immutable characteristics (race + gender) and disregards their behavior or worldviews. It sends the message to women and anyone who's not white that they will always be victims. That's not unifying or empowering; that's robbing individuals of their agency.

- Stating that upper/middle class individuals are economically abusive promotes one class of people over another. This is discrimination. It's another predetermined judgment that sends a message to financially poor individuals that they are victims, always will be, and that upper/middle class individuals are the abusers.

- Stating that heterosexuals are abusers of the LGBTQ+ community promotes LGBTQ+ individuals over heterosexuals. This is discrimination. It draws predetermined, harmful, and hateful conclusions of people based solely on their sexual orientation. This sends the message that individuals that identify as LGBTQ+ are constant victims and must always be afraid of heterosexuals, and that heterosexuals are abusers just because of their sexual orientation. It is wrong to draw blanket conclusions about people in this way.

- Stating that Christians are abusers of non-Christians promotes other religions over Christianity. That's religious discrimination. It draws predetermined, harmful, and hateful conclusions of people based solely on their religious views. And again, it sends the message to non-Christians that they will always be victims. They, too, are robbed of their agency.

- Stating that Native English Speakers use status over Non-Native English Speakers promotes one group of individuals over another simply based on their native language. An individual has no control over where they're born or what language they learn first, yet those born in an English-speaking location are guilty, nonetheless. This is another predetermined and divisive judgement being promulgated by the school system.

This training tells students and teachers that being white is bad, being a man is bad, being straight is bad, being a Christian is bad, saving money is bad, speaking English is bad, living without a disability is bad. By default, this training also tells children that it's better if you're not white, it's better if you're a woman, it's better if you're gay or transgender, it's better if you're not a Christian, it's better if you're a socialist or Marxist, it's better if you're not a native English speaker, and it's better if you're disabled. And even then, you're still the "marginalized" group — you're always the victim. How's a child ever supposed to feel good about himself or herself? How are children supposed to be friends if they're taught to hate each other — that their class members are going to abuse and oppress them? How's anyone going to be encouraged in life if they're always told they're a victim and that the circumstances of their victimhood are completely out of their control? How can anyone achieve success if they're taught that they'll never make it because society is out to get them?

These messages are damaging to children on both sides of the "oppressor" and "oppressed" categorization, especially when they are taught to children as fact, not theory.

By stating that straight men are oppressive and abusive toward homosexuals, Chicago Public Schools (CPS) incentivizes young boys to become homosexual (i.e., not oppressive). By stating that men are oppressors, CPS incentivizes young boys to identify as a female. In just one training video, CPS is pushing Critical Race Theory, Gender Theory, and the LGBTQ+ agenda on thousands of teachers and students. How many more schools are teaching the same stuff?

To make any of these assertions is extremely prejudicial, racist, and discriminatory, and Chicago Public Schools is guilty on all counts. CPS is teaching its employees and students (particularly the white, male, Christian, heterosexuals) to hate themselves and hate each other based on traits they have no control over (race, gender, disability). It incentivizes students to identify as victims because it's better than being an oppressor. It locks them into a life of perpetual victimhood because the students are taught that they were born with their victimhood status and it is completely out of their control.

And more than that, this mindset disincentives students from engaging in the learning process, from putting the effort into the thing — education — that could help true victims out of their victimhood status. Why work hard to excel at math if the system is rigged against you? Why study hard to earn an A in biology and dream of becoming a doctor someday if you'll never make it because everyone is out to get you? Rather than provide students with the tools to achieve big dreams, better their lives, and take care of their families, these materials hurt students and cheat them out of their best opportunity to get ahead.

According to Chicago Public Schools, I (and perhaps many others reading this book) am considered an oppressor, an abuser, an intimidator, a threat, and a minimizer simply because I am a heterosexual, English speaking, white, Christian, middle-class, non-disabled man in my thirties. Would the same be said of a female Muslim of color or a transgender youth who is an atheist? According to the CPS mandatory training, no, of course not — that's impossible.

I was extremely uncomfortable with this training — and even more uncomfortable with the idea that this could ever be taught to young children in their formative years, and particularly without parental knowledge or consent. Think of the impact this has on children. They're taught to judge a person (and themselves), not on the content of their character, but on their color of skin, sex, religion, income level, age, language, and physical ability. It made me feel unwelcome in my community and my workplace. I could only assume that my bosses and coworkers believed evil, detrimental things about me apart and aside from my professional behavior, skills, and abilities.

To be clear, this training perpetuates the very things the it claims to be fighting against — racism, prejudice, and discrimination. The Merriam-Webster Dictionary defines these words as follows:

- *Racism:* a belief that race is a fundamental determinant of human traits and capacities and that racial differences produce an inherent superiority of a particular race.
- *Prejudice:* preconceived judgment or opinion; an adverse opinion or leaning formed without just grounds or before sufficient knowledge; an irrational attitude of hostility directed against an individual, a group, a race, or their supposed characteristics.

- *Discrimination:* prejudiced or prejudicial outlook, action, or treatment; the act, practice, or an instance of discriminating categorically rather than individually.

If I were to agree and comply with the content of this mandatory training, then I would also have to agree with the following two statements:

1. I would have to believe that one race, gender, or class is better than another and that these characteristics predetermine the outcome of a person's life.
2. I would begin to shame myself and others like me because of my many alleged acts of abuse, manipulations, threats, and oppression. I would have to acknowledge my guilt of being white ... being a man ... being straight ... being a Christian.... I simply must hate myself for existing.

CRITICAL RACE THEORY

Critical Race Theory ("CRT") teaches that race is the most critical feature of an individual and that society should be viewed through a racial lens. CRT divides America into two groups: *oppressors* and *victims,* arguing that whites are the oppressors and non-whites are the victims; it's inherently a Marxist theory based entirely on race. Marxism largely focuses on social class, whereas Critical Race Theory teaches that race determines one's social class. The two ideologies pit two groups against each other through racist, prejudiced, and discriminatory beliefs.

> *Critical Race Theory ("CRT") teaches that race is the most critical feature of an individual and that society should be viewed through a racial lens.*

The definition of Critical Race Theory according to *Critical Race Training in Education* is as follows:

> Critical Race Theory ... is a radical ideology that focuses on race as the key to understanding society, and objectifies people based on race. An outgrowth of the European Marxist school of critical theory, critical race theory is an academic movement which seeks to link racism, race, and power. Unlike the Civil Rights movement, which sought to work within the structures of American democracy, critical race theorists challenge the very foundations of the liberal order, such as rationalism, constitutional law, and legal reasoning. Critical race theorists argue that American social life, political structures, and economic systems are founded upon race, which (in their view) is a social construct. ... Systemic racism, in the eyes of critical race theorists, stems from the dominance of race in American life. Critical race theorists and anti-racist advocates argue that, because race is a predominant part of American life, racism itself has become internalized into the American conscience.[2]

CRT is "An outgrowth of the European Marxist school of critical theory." Make no mistake about it, Critical Race Theory is openly and intentionally a Marxist ideology with the end goal always set on communism and the destruction of constitutional law. There are nine methods, and examples, used to implement CRT in universities, colleges, and even public schools:

1. Changing Admissions Policies
   It's common practice among American universities to prioritize the race of an applicant as opposed to his or her academic performance, all in the name of "equity."

---

2. criticalrace.org.

2. Implementing Anti-Racism, Bias, and Diversity Training
    a. The "Intersecting Identities" graphic used in my CPS training is an example of how this goal is achieved in K–12 schools. It teaches that only white people have bias and that they all have the same bias against the same people (monolithic), as opposed to all people having some sort of bias, regardless of race.
    b. This sounds good in theory but is deceptive; it uses actual racism to "fight" perceived racism.
3. Changing Curriculum Requirements
    a. The "No Zero Policy," as used in my former school district, would give students scores no lower than a 50%, effectively lowering performance standards for all students. The installation of *Common Core* is an example of this strategy.
    b. Mao closed schools for a year in communist China to implement an entirely new curriculum. Teachers that did not agree with the curriculum were removed.
    c. Nazi Germany used this method to indoctrinate the Hitler Youth.
    d. To rid itself of "white language supremacy," an Arizona State University professor proposed using "labor-based grading," which rewards effort as opposed to quality work.[3] This means having the correct answers is not as important as trying.
4. Instituting Disciplinary Measures
    A seven-year-old girl in Mission Viejo, California, was reprimanded in school for drawing a

---

3. https://www.foxnews.com/us/arizona-state-professor-white-language-supremacy-labor-based-grading.

picture containing the words "Any life matters" underneath the BLM slogan. The little girl was forced to sit out from recess, made to apologize to her class, and told that she can no longer draw pictures in school.[4]

5. Politically Supporting Anti-Racist Activism
BLM holds school events through their "BLM at School" initiative; some activities include affirming transgender people, celebrating George Floyd's birthday, and calling for defunding the police.[5]

6. Funding CRT Programs and Research
In the middle of the Covid pandemic, Chicago Public Schools received $1.8 billion from the federal American Rescue Plan in 2021. These funds will be used for CPS's "Moving Forward Together" plan.[6]

7. "Re-imagining" Policing
BLM calls to defund the police departments to fund education.

8. Providing Anti-Racist Resources
Teacher trainings are, perhaps, the most efficient and effective way these resources are provided to teachers and students.

9. Taking "Symbolic" Actions
Removing historic statues, renaming buildings, celebrating Gay Pride month, and observing the International Transgender Day of Visibility.

These methods of implementing CRT are very prevalent in the education system; several of these methods were even used in the mandatory staff trainings I experienced while teaching for Chicago Public Schools. The breakdown of family values

4. https://go2tutors.com/student-punished-black-lives-matter/.
5. https://www.blacklivesmatteratschool.com/year-of-purpose.html.
6. https://www.cps.edu/strategic-initiatives/moving-forward-together/).

and the removal of God in America allowed for this indoctrination process to begin, though at a slow pace initially. The pace, however, has hit warp speed and is uprooting traditional values, not just in universities, but in K–12 schools across the country. A fight to stop this destructive process from the inside out would be a long fight, maybe longer than we can afford. Bringing education back home is the best and most effective way to build up the next generation and set them on solid ground — spiritually, emotionally, mentally, and academically.

> Finally, brethren, whatsoever things are true, whatsoever things are honest, whatsoever things are just, whatsoever things are pure, whatsoever things are lovely, whatsoever things are of good report; if there be any virtue, and if there be any praise, think on these things. — Philippians 4:8

The choice to homeschool is not a defeated move or removal from society, it's simply a move toward that which is true, honest, just, pure, lovely, good, virtuous, and full of praise.

GENDER THEORY

Unfortunately, CRT was not the only controversial aspect of my mandatory training at Chicago Public Schools. The mandatory teacher trainings I experienced also included many segments on Gender Theory, another theory rooted in Marxism that pits groups of people against each other and ultimately desires the dismantling of the entire system in the name of "equity." Gender Theory asserts that gender is a social construct, something made up by society, and is not the same thing as biological sex. For example, Gender Theory states that a biological boy can be a girl, a biological girl can be a boy, and that gender can change back and forth. Gender

Theory also states that one's gender may depend on their race, ethnicity, religion, age, or health status.[7]

Gender Dysphoria, which is different from Gender Theory, can be described as when a person's thoughts and feelings don't line up with their gender (i.e., a girl trapped in a boy's body). A phenomenon called Rapid Onset Gender Dysphoria (ROGD) is when an individual has no signs or history of gender confusion and then, seemingly overnight, they begin to identify as transgender.[8] This trend is increasingly common with teenagers, especially in female friend groups, and has been heavily linked to increased use of social media.

- In the last decade, adolescent girls have gone from the extreme minority to the overwhelming majority, in terms of cases of gender dysphoria.[9]
  - Historically, the incidence of gender dysphoria for boys has been .005–.014 and for girls it has been .002–.003 (less than 1 in 10,000).

- As of 2017, 2% of all high school students identify as "transgender" (a 1000% increase).

- For four consecutive generations, the number of people identifying as LGBTQ has roughly doubled compared to the previous generation.
  - Gen Z (born 1997–2012): 20.8%
  - Millennials (born 1981–1996): 10.5%
  - Gen X (born 1965–1980): 4.2%
  - Baby boomers (born 1946–1964): 2.6%
  - Traditionalists (born before 1946): 0.8%

In the same "Intersectionality" video that contained the "Intersecting Identities" graphic,[10] CPS presented a slide illustrating

---

7. https://www.ohchr.org/EN/Issues/SexualOrientationGender/Pages/GenderTheory.aspx.
8. https://www.dailywire.com/news/sociological-contagion-and-the-growing-non-binary-movement.
9. Abigail Shrier, *Irreversible Damage* (Washington, DC: Regnery Publ.), p. 32.
10. https://www.youtube.com/watch?v=alukdZlrDp4).

one of its own transgender students named Ember (not the student's real name)— a biological boy identifying as a girl. It was titled, "Intersectionality Activity: This is Ember (she/her)." The slide contained four bullet points of information regarding Ember: 1) Ember was an 8th grade student in Chicago Public Schools, 2) Ember was a black, trans girl, 3) Ember was the only out transgender person in school, and 4) Ember is out as transgender at school but not at home. This is a loaded slide and deserves to be unpacked. Applying logic and objectivity, one can come to the following conclusions:

- The school knows that the student, a minor, is hiding their transgender identity from their parents.
- The school is referring to a male student as a female, without parental knowledge or consent.
- The school acknowledges that this minor student is publicly "out" as transgender.
- The school has not communicated any of this to the student's parents.

The image presents a seriously big problem. According to CPS, Ember is 13 or 14 years old and is "out to her school but not her family." This means that Ember leaves home each morning as a boy, walks into school, identifies as a girl, and is treated by administrators, teachers, and classmates as, a girl. Ember's classmates know what's going on, the teachers know what's going on, and the principal knows what's going on; they all refer to Ember as a girl throughout the school day, yet Ember's family has no idea about any of it. Nobody tells the parents?! And let's not forget that Ember is a minor, and yet the parents are intentionally shut out and kept in the dark in terms of Ember's life at school. And this process is actively promoted in the mandatory teacher trainings as a good thing — the teachers must "protect" Ember from Ember's own parents because the parents are a threat and unaffirming. After all, the school knows Ember better than Ember's own parents, right?! This is a form of child abuse taking place on school grounds, every day, by adults, in secret.

> If a student cusses in school, parents get a call.
>
> If a student gets in a fight, parents get a call.
>
> If a student gets a tummy ache, parents get a call.
>
> If a student misses an assignment, parents get a call.
>
> If a student gets a headache and wants an aspirin, parents get a call.
>
> If a student changes their identity and is a victim of sexual, mental, and emotional abuse at school, DON'T TELL THE PARENTS!

This is an example of the state superseding parental rights and exerting parental authority over a minor — facilitated by the public school system and paid for by your tax dollars. Schools should not be intentionally keeping things from parents, especially if a child is undergoing major physical, mental, and emotional stress like gender dysphoria (assuming each case actually involves gender dysphoria, as opposed to merely participating in a social contagion, as many opine is actually occurring in classrooms today). That is exactly the kind of stress that requires parental support and guidance. This type of secrecy and allegiance to the state undermines the sanctity of the family unit and ultimately hurts the child who needs his or her parents. In fact, creating an ideological separation between children and their parents was a tactic used by Nazi Germany when forming the *Hitler Youth*.

When Hitler came to power in the 1930s, he led a concerted effort to persuade the youth to adopt the principles of National Socialism (Nazi-ism). Concerning this effort, Adolf Hitler once wrote to a friend:

> Children have been deliberately taken away from parents who refused to acknowledge their belief in National Socialism. The refusal of parents to allow their

children to join the youth organization is regarded as an adequate reason for taking the children away.[11]

Students in Nazi Germany were encouraged to report if their own parents were or were not Nazi supporters, thus pitting parents and children against each other. In less than a decade of Hitler's indoctrination of youth in schools, the Nazi party began the murder of six-million Jews in the Holocaust. To be able to draw any sort of parallel between Hitler's Nazi Germany and our public school system is mind-boggling. We need to course correct or, better yet, get on a whole new course before it's too late.

Following is a graphic from Chicago Public Schools mandatory staff training in 2020.[12] This image is from a training video called "What Does Transgender Mean?"[13]

Source: Graphic by TSER, Trans Student Educational Resources, 2015, http://www.transstudent.org/gender. Used by CC BY 4.0. https://creativecommons.org/licenses/by/4.0/.

---

11. https://spartacus-educational.com/GEReducation.htm.
12. https://www.youtube.com/watch?v=DmOEwcmU_Ic.
13. Trans Student Educational Resources, 2015. "The Gender Unicorn," http://www.transstudent.org/gender.

In the video, the narrator promotes this "Gender Unicorn" as "adorable" and recommends that teachers use this image in their classrooms; there's even an interactive version available online. The narrator further states, "You do have to respect the language that people use for themselves." This means if a five-year-old girl in kindergarten says one day that she's a boy, school staff should "respect the language" she's using for herself and refer to her as a boy. CPS did not ask parents for permission to show this graphic in kindergarten classrooms. It was simply given to teachers who were then encouraged to share with students — kept behind the curtain and snuck in through the proverbial back door. By the time parents could find out what's being taught in the classroom, it's too late. Remember, this training took place mid-year during Covid when everyone was fully remote. That means no print-offs, no handouts, no packages being sent home for parents to review and/or approve. These are images and topics that could be flashed on-screen during the online class meeting and taken off in an instant. This is a clear example of the sexualization of children that's taking place on a massive scale, carried out by public schools, and paid for by your tax dollars.

For nearly a decade, I was the only male P.E. teacher at my school in Indiana. Naturally, I was asked to supervise the "puberty video" shown to fourth grade boys each year. For students to watch this video, their parents were required to sign and return a permission slip. Fathers could even choose to come to the school and sit in on the video themselves; mothers held the same right for their daughters. The video would talk about the body changing and growing, muscles getting bigger and growing more body hair. Sexuality and gender were never discussed — and that was fourth graders! Now, schools are teaching five-year-olds about gender identity, sexual attraction, and homosexuality without parental consent.

In the same mandatory staff training as the aforementioned "Gender Unicorn," Chicago Public Schools presented statistics on the sexual orientation of its own students. According to

Student Sexual identity in the Chicago Public High Schools:
2020

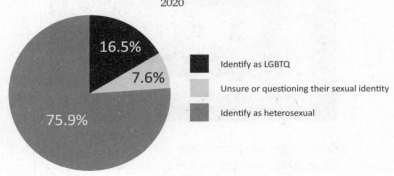

16.5%

7.6%

75.9%

Identify as LGBTQ

Unsure or questioning their sexual identity

Identify as heterosexual

2020 data, 16.5% of high school students in Chicago Public Schools identified as LGBTQ while 7.6% were questioning their sexual or gender identity — that's almost 25% of the high school population in Chicago! That means one out of every four students in Chicago is either gay, transgender, or unsure if they're gay or transgender. If those numbers seem uniquely high, it's because they are.

While 16–24% of the high school population in Chicago identifies as LGBTQ, the percentage across the rest of the U.S. is only 5.6%.[14] Why is the rate among the high school population in Chicago at least 3–5 times higher than the national average?

- The number of people identifying as LGBTQ in America has nearly doubled in the last decade.

- The number of high school students that have considered suicide increased 25% between 2009 and 2017.

- Cases of clinical depression among teens increased 37% between 2005 and 2014.

- Girls are experiencing depression at three times the rate of boys.

---

14. https://news.gallup.com/poll/332522/percentage-americans-lgbt.aspx.

- Reports of self-harm have increased 62% overall since 2009, the spike entirely attributed to girls.

- Rates of self-harm among 10-year-old to 14-year-old girls have nearly tripled in the last 15 years.[15]

Above is an example of materials that CPS passed out to students in elementary and middle school. The image is of materials that were distributed throughout my school in Chicago at the beginning of June 2021 in celebration of "Gay Pride Month."

The "everyone is welcome here" sign was given to teachers who were encouraged to display the sign on their classroom doors. In addition to the sign, the entire school (students included) was given two pins to wear in support of the Gay and Trans movements. Kindergarten students were even given wristbands with the transgender flag colors. Just to summarize, Bibles can't be distributed even on a voluntarily basis, but gay and trans paraphernalia are distributed without request, celebrated en masse, and teachers and students are coerced into participation. This is yet another example of the sexualization of children carried out by public schools and with your tax dollars. The school administration not only distributed these materials, but they encouraged teachers and students to display and wear them, which many did. What if I chose not to display the sign on my door or wear the pins? It's not like I had ever denied students entry to my classroom

---

15. Shrier, *Irreversible Damage*, p. 32.

before, and certainly not because of their sexual orientation. In fact, for many years I displayed a pineapple on my door as a sign of welcome and hospitality. I never spoke to my students (who were all young children) about sexual orientation, and it would've been extremely inappropriate if I had. These materials serve as identifiers, pointing out supporters and non-supporters. Again, instead of unity we are separated into two opposing groups.

Some teachers gave students LGBTQ bracelets in class where students drew pictures and letters saying, "Happy pride!" Students as young as five years old were giving me "Pride Pictures" they had drawn in class. What does a five-year-old know about homosexuality, being transgender, gender dysphoria, or sex in general? And who is teaching them this stuff? Why is this being pushed on children and where are the parents?!

WORDS HAVE MEANING

Marxist/Communist regimes, through history, controlled language and changed the meaning of words to gain influence and power. Public schools in America are controlling speech to alter history and fundamentally change America. School systems, along with media propaganda, have proven to be the most efficient and effective way for Marxist/Communist regimes to control people — Hitler did it, Mao did it, Kim Jong-un is doing it, and America's public schools are doing it, too.

Mandatory teacher trainings are a quiet and discreet way that public schools can implement controversial policies on Gender Theory and Critical Race Theory in America's classrooms. Students as young as kindergarten (often

> *Marxist/Communist regimes, through history, controlled language and changed the meaning of words to gain influence and power. Public schools in America are controlling speech to alter history and fundamentally change America.*

younger) are being taught about homosexual attraction and are shown explicit sexual images that are first given to their teachers during mandatory teacher trainings. For example, "Drag Queen Hour" has become popular for the youngest grade levels, and even field trips to gay bars so that children can watch Drag Queens perform under neon signs that say things like "It's not going to lick itself."[16] The transgender movement, which has absolutely skyrocketed since the mid-2000s, is an example of how language manipulation can control the population. Through the transgender movement, the words "man" and "woman" have begun to lose meaning. The term "Toxic Masculinity" is used to degrade men and "Birthing Persons" is used to replace women.

The concrete and immutable characteristics that have distinguished men from women since creation are now being replaced by feelings and emotion. If the definitions of the words "male" and "female" can be changed, then anything can be changed; truth and fact do not exist — everything is subjective. This is the opposite of what education should be — a process that relies on objective truth and fact.

16. https://www.dailywire.com/news/florida-school-takes-elementary-school-children-on-field-trip-to-gay-bar.

The case of Peter Vlaming is just one recent example of the dangerous impact that controlling language and words can have on society. Peter Vlaming was a French teacher at West Point High School in West Point, Virginia. He was fired from his position in 2018 after refusing to refer to a transgender student by their preferred pronouns. Mr. Vlaming taught the student, a biological female, for two years prior to the student making the transition from female to male. After meetings with the student, the student's parents, and the school principal about the issue, Mr. Vlaming still refused to use masculine pronouns for a biological female, despite receiving orders from school administration to do so. Mr. Vlaming believed that referring to a biological girl as a boy was a lie and doing so would violate his religion and right to free speech. If words like "man" and "woman" no longer have meaning, and speech can be compelled by the state, then we no longer have a free society. The oligarchy in charge of the country gets to determine what words mean, when the meanings can change, and who gets to say what. Words have meaning. Words matter. If this fight is not won, then Liberty is lost.[17]

My comments on Gender Theory are not meant to eradicate the topic from schools. My belief is that parents should have the final say on *how* and *when* the discussion takes place in schools. I believe there's a time and place to discuss most anything, but when morality, religion, sexuality, or other sensitive topics are in play, the default response should always go to the parents. If parents can sign permission slips for their child to go on a field trip, then parents can sign a permission slip for their child to learn about Gender Theory — as long as it's done on the parents' terms. The teaching of Gender Theory in public schools accomplishes at least four of the *Communist Goals to take over America*. They are:

1. *Get control of the schools. Use them as transmission belts for socialism and current Communist propaganda.*

---

17. https://www.washingtonpost.com/nation/2019/10/01/virginia-teacher-fired-not-using-transgender-pronouns-sues-school/.

Soften the curriculum. Get control of teachers' associations. Put the party line in textbooks.
a. Public schools are transmission belts for promoting Gender Theory through mandatory staff trainings.

2. *Eliminate all laws governing obscenity by calling them "censorship" and a violation of free speech and free press.*
    a. Schools that teach kindergartners about Gender Theory and homosexuality are normalizing the sexualization of children.

3. *Break down cultural standards of morality by promoting pornography and obscenity in books, magazines, motion pictures, radio, and TV.*
    a. The "Gender Unicorn" being used to teach kindergartners about gender identity and homosexuality is one example of the breakdown of cultural standards and promotion of obscenity.

4. *Present homosexuality, degeneracy, and promiscuity as "normal, natural, healthy."*
    a. Schools present the LGBTQ lifestyle as normal, natural, and healthy through mandatory staff trainings and the forced celebration of Gay Pride month.
    b. As the family unit breaks down and is further divided from biblical morality, schools and other LGBTQ allies become the pseudo-family. A similar tactic was used by dictators and totalitarian leaders during the 20th century to expand their power and influence.

One example of the prevalence and impact of Gender Theory in schools comes from the state of Maryland. Maryland's largest school district saw a 582% increase in students that identify as non-binary from 2020-2022. In Montgomery County Schools, a total of 423 students across 84 schools, including 20 elementary schools, completed an intake form at the beginning of the school year answering questions about their gender identity, preferred pronouns, and how they would rank their parental support. According to the results, 45% of students identified as non-binary, which was an increase of nearly 600% over a two year period; the largest increase was among middle school students.[18] In addition, Montgomery County School District guidelines state that students have a right to keep their in-school gender identities private and that parents do not have a right to be involved if the student says they're not supportive at home.[19] This is yet another example of schools promoting the LGBTQ ideology while simultaneously and intentionally keeping parents in the dark.

The rise of Gender Theory tears down societal and cultural norms, defies biological fact, and promotes the sexualization of children, all of which promote the rise of godlessness in America. If that sounds too far-fetched or overstated, just ask yourself how we got to the point as a society where Disney now offers to pay for sex-change surgeries for children of its employees, the American Library Association hosted Drag Queen Story Hours for toddlers, men can give birth, and your pronouns can be "zhe/zhir/zhirs/zhirself." Some apt descriptions may be "craze," "social contagion," and "mass formation psychosis."

> And even as they did not like to retain God in *their* knowledge, God gave them over to a reprobate mind, to do those things which are not convenient. — Romans 1:28

---

18. (https://dailycaller.com/2022/10/11/maryland-schools-spike-reported-gender-confused-trans-montgomery-county/.

19. https://www.montgomeryschoolsmd.org/uploadedFiles/students/rights/0504.21_GenderIdentityGuidelinesForStudents_Web.pdf.

The only hope we have is a spiritual awakening — a return to God and truth. Public schools are not teaching, and will not teach biblical truth, so it's incumbent upon parents to take on the task — homeschooling provides the perfect platform.

5

My Conflict as a Christian Teaching in a Public School

It is becoming more and more difficult for Christian parents to send their kids to a public school. I have described several common public school policies that are not compatible with Christianity or the Bible. Children as young as pre-k and kindergarten are being taught about Gender Theory and Critical Race Theory, while they're still so young and impressionable. The problem is not so much *what* is being taught, it's *how* and *when* it's being taught. Gender Theory and Critical Race Theory are just that, theories. However, they're being presented as fact to vulnerable children incapable of critical thought and lacking the ability to process such complicated material. And if a student, parent, or teacher were to speak out in opposition to these ideologies, it's labeled as hate speech, racist, or bigoted. It seems that diversity and tolerance seem to provide space for any and everything in today's culture, except Christian values.

As a Christian, I hold a biblical worldview and maintain traditional American values, both of which are at odds with the current progressive educational system. Schools are trading "all men are created equal" for "white people are privileged and people of color are marginalized." "In God We Trust" is being replaced with Critical Race Theory. "E Pluribus Unum" is turning into "oppressor vs. oppressed" and "life, liberty, and the pursuit of happiness" is morphing into "redistribution of wealth." Whether in a small town or big city, if you hold a biblical worldview and adhere to Christian principles, then a conflict of values with your local school system and school board is inevitable and imminent.

The teaching profession is an increasingly liberal profession, and the divide is even greater at the collegiate level where liberal professors outnumber their conservative counterparts 12:1.

Chicago Public Schools is the third-largest school system in America, behind New York City and Los Angeles. Chicago Public School board members have been appointed for over 150 years — appointed, not elected. The city's mayor is responsible for appointing CPS board members; Chicago has not had a Republican mayor in over 90 years. Safe to say, the city of Chicago leans very left on the political spectrum, generally speaking. Chicago certainly is not unique in this regard; many other cities have a similar story. The teaching profession is an increasingly liberal profession, and the divide is even greater at the collegiate level where liberal professors outnumber their conservative counterparts 12:1.[1]

The trainings described in the previous chapter took place in the middle of the school year, so the second half of the school year was an internal battle for me. I stood in disagreement with the ideologies that CPS was implementing, but what could I have done about it? What *should* I have done about it? These were questions I struggled with for months. On one hand, I loved teaching and coaching. It

---

1. https://www.washingtontimes.com/news/2016/oct/6/liberal-profes-
   sors-outnumber-conservatives-12-1/).

comes naturally to me and I can do it well. I went to school to be a teacher and I worked hard to become a better teacher and coach. I have made friends and wonderful memories in this field. I had prayed for each position I held and thanked God for every opportunity I was given; I did not want to walk away from things God had blessed me with. On the other hand, I could not implement the ideologies that my employer was asking me to implement. I could not, in good conscience, teach my students what I felt to be lies, nor could I participate in something that I felt to be in direct contradiction to my Christian faith.

The following two verses sum up the conflict I was having both as a Christian and as a public school teacher.

- "We ought to obey God rather than men." — Acts 5:29
- "Let every soul be subject unto the higher powers. For there is no power but of God: the powers that be are ordained of God." — Romans 13:1

These two verses seem to pull in opposite directions, but how could these two, seemingly conflicting Scriptures, both be true at the same time? As a teacher, I want to be a good employee. I want my principal to like me and give me good performance reviews. I want my colleagues and students to like and respect me. As a Christian, I want to obey the Word of God. I want to be led by the Holy Spirit and be a faithful follower of Christ. Is there a way to obey God *and* be subject to man at the same time? Certainly, I am not the first person to ever encounter this sort of spiritual conflict and I'm certain I will not be the last. While my role was as a teacher, there are countless administrators, parents, and students facing the same conflict I did. Obeying God doesn't mean we should defy our boss or quit our job every time there's a problem, and being subject to authority doesn't mean blind obedience, regardless of what the Word of God says.

It was difficult to know what the appropriate response should've been. Should I compromise my Christian convictions and do what the school says because it's just a job? Should I hold to my convictions, stand in opposition to my school, and risk being ostracized, suspended, or accused of hate speech? I'm not advocating for isolation, avoiding conflict, or avoiding diversity of thought. Actually, quite the opposite — Christians are called to be light and salt in the world — to be *in* the world but not *of* the world. Christians should always look at things through a spiritual lens and weigh everything against the Word of God. So, when my employer told its employees that white, Christian men are privileged and abusive simply because they're white, Christian men, I recalled what the Bible says:

> There is nether Jew nor Greek, there is neither bond nor free, there is neither male nor female: for ye are all one in Christ Jesus. — Galatians 3:28

The Bible places all men and women as equal, and that no race, class, or gender is preferred above another, while many public schools are teaching that certain races, classes, and genders are better or worse than others. The Bible got it right, man gets it wrong. Public schools are teaching that race, class, and gender are what determines one's character, making some "privileged" and others "marginalized." This teaching is wrong. It is not godly. It is racist, prejudiced, and discriminatory.

When your school teaches that you're abusive to children and women just because you exist in the body you were given, and that you're oppressive toward people of a different race — will you choose to stay in that school?

When your school teaches that you're a victim if you're female, disabled, homosexual, transgender, not white, or not a Christian — will you choose to stay in that school?

When your school teaches that boys (especially white boys) are abusive and oppressive toward girls — will you choose to stay in that school?

When your school promotes and incentivizes the sexualization of children as young as five years old — will you choose to stay in that school?

When your school says a biological girl must be called a boy in your class, that you're legally obligated to call her a boy — will you choose to stay in that school?

When your school says you cannot notify parents if their child has a secret sexual orientation or gender identity in school — will you choose to stay in that school?

After reading a list like that you might think, "Why in the world would anyone choose to be in a school like that?"

Part of me wanted to be like Daniel in the lion's den, David facing Goliath, and the three Hebrew youth in the fiery furnace. Not to inflate myself, but I believed that God could protect me in this environment and use me even under the worst circumstances, just like those stories in the Bible. The other part of me wanted to be like Lot fleeing the city before certain destruction. This is the conflict I believe so many families are going through, particularly Christian families. Do you keep your kids in public schools and trust the Lord to protect them? Or do you remove your kids from public schools and leave before total destruction? Should you stay or should you go?

John the Baptist cried in the wilderness, "Prepare ye the way of the Lord" (Matthew 3:3), and he confronted Herod concerning his unlawful marriage. Moses told the people, "Stand still, and see the salvation of the LORD. … the LORD shall fight for you, and ye shall hold your peace" (Exodus 14:13–14). Do I stand up for the Word of God and confront the school board members or do I hold my peace and let the Lord fight for me?

God sent Jonah to call Nineveh to repentance; He didn't send anyone else — just Jonah. When Jonah ran away, God didn't just move on to plan B and call someone else to Nineveh. God dealt with Jonah in a unique way and Jonah eventually did obey God, resulting in the entire city of Nineveh being saved!

All Christians want to be used by God to accomplish a great work or see a great miracle. We see so many examples in the Bible where just one faithful servant is used to accomplish a mighty work of God — we all want that powerful testimony. However, God uses individuals in different ways. The way God would use one person may look completely different from the way God would use me or you. There will be times when God says to go and there will be times when God says to stay. If God does say go, then you better go — think of Jonah. If God says to stay, then you better stay — think of the fiery furnace or the Disciples on the Day of Pentecost. There are biblical examples of both staying and leaving, resting and fighting, speaking and holding your tongue. They seem to contradict each other, but they don't. Ecclesiastes 3:1 says, "To every thing there is a season, and a time to every purpose under the heaven."

We also can find many examples in the Bible when a child of God acts out of presumption and not according to God's Word. Acting on presumption is a huge mistake, one that so many believers (myself included) have made before. God promised a child to Abraham and Sarah, so they thought they were doing God's work by using Hagar to bear Abraham's son instead of waiting on God's promise. Abraham and Sarah acted out of presumption and made a mess of things. They knew what God had said but took the wrong actions. Eventually, Abraham and Sarah were obedient to God's Word and Sarah conceived Isaac, as God had promised.

If God tells you to go, then go. If God says to stay, then stay. If God says to speak, then speak.

It sounds simple but it can be an agonizing process. A personal relationship with God Almighty is the greatest solution any of us can have. As Christians, we all need to seek God for ourselves. We need to hear from God for ourselves. We all must be in relationship with Him. Reading His Word. Praying constantly. Praising Him and thanking Him. Asking for wisdom. Asking for the guidance of the Holy Spirit. Listening to Him. Following Him. Jesus said, "My sheep hear my voice, and I know them, and they follow me" (John 10:27). Hear Him, know Him, and follow Him.

At this point, it still may be unclear which path to take. How should a Christian respond to the indoctrination taking place in public schools? The teacher in me says that if I have a complaint, I should offer a solution. So, what is my proposed solution? For my parents and for me, homeschooling was the solution, but only because our education was rooted in God's Word. If I had been given a secular homeschool education, similar to what I would've received in public school, I don't know if I'd be a Christian today, I highly doubt that I would've left my job with Chicago Public Schools, and I definitely wouldn't be writing this book. So, if you can, homeschool your kids and give them an education with a biblical worldview.

FULL CIRCLE

After one year of teaching for Chicago Public Schools, I prayerfully decided to file a formal complaint with the school board and resign from my teaching position. I left Chicago Public Schools because they were implementing ideologies that were contrary to the Word of God and discriminated against its students and employees based on their race, sex, sexual orientation, and religion. I did not want to be associated with a system like that and could not, in good conscience, continue to work there. I did receive a response from the Chicago Public School Board concerning my formal complaint. In their response, I was notified that there would not be an investigation into the matter at this time. Basically, the school board decided not to investigate themselves. Does anyone else see a problem with that? "The Great Oz has spoken! Pay no attention to that man behind the curtain."

Make no mistake about it — this was a very difficult decision to make. If you're a parent, making difficult decisions is part of the job. Conflict is a part of life and I certainly don't believe a person should quit every time there's a problem — you'd never get anything done. My background in homeschooling and the biblical education I received from my parents gave me a firm foundation to stand on when making such a difficult decision. I hope to encourage parents and assure them that their actions matter to their kids. Your kids are watching and what you teach them will stick with them. That certainly was the case for me.

I already explained the reasons why my parents decided to homeschool my three older siblings and me — to raise us up in the fear and admonition of the Lord. They were concerned with the Indiana Supreme Court's decision to stop the Gideons from distributing Bibles in schools. My parents prioritized the Word of God, they stood up for the Bible in their hometown, and defended the Gospel on national television. They may have just been trying to do what they believed to be right, but more importantly, they showed their kids how to live for God. It's not easy. It takes prayer. It takes reading the Bible. It takes patience. It takes courage and faith to act. My parents did not homeschool their children perfectly, neither will you, and neither will anybody else. But God is good and loving and He wants us closer to Him as He guides us along.

When I finally made the decision to leave my job as a public school teacher and file a formal complaint, I was reminded of my mom's letter to the editor and my parents' decision to homeschool. It was a full circle moment for me. I was still learning from my parents and following the example they set over 30 years ago. Like my parents — I wanted to prioritize the Word of God, I wrote a letter, stood on biblical values, and left public schools to develop homeschool curriculum. Just weeks after my resignation from CPS, I was fortunate enough to launch my first course in the Master Books Academy. Along with my return to homeschooling came the opportunity and freedom to teach with a biblical worldview. I'm completely confident that I made the right decision and thankful that I was able to return to my homeschool roots.

6

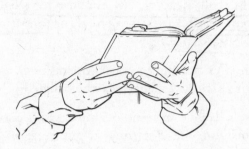

The Bible's Role in Education

Since before the founding of the United States, our leaders placed a premium on a moral and virtuous education, believing that an educated public is a prerequisite to self-governance.

> "If the children are untaught, their ignorance and vices will in future life cost us much dearer in their consequences than it would have done in their correction by a good education." — Thomas Jefferson[1]

> "If virtue and knowledge are diffused among the people, they will never be enslaved. This will be their great security." — Samuel Adams[2]

The Bible was the principal text in schools for much of America's history, when virtue and wisdom were taught. For decades now, the First Amendment has been misused to keep Bibles and Christian morals out of public schools. For clarity, let's look to Fisher Ames, the man who actually wrote the First Amendment.

---

1. http://jti.lib.virginia.edu/jefferson/quotations/jeff1350.htm.
2. https://www.nas.org/blogs/article/u_s_founding_fathers_on_education_in_their_own_words.

Fisher Ames was a Congressman from Massachusetts during the first session of Congress in 1789 and is credited with wording the First Amendment, which reads:

> Congress shall make no law establishing religion, or to prevent the free exercise thereof, or to infringe the rights of conscience.

One month after crafting the First Amendment, Ames wrote an article for *Palladium* magazine, which stated:

> We have a dangerous trend beginning to take place in our education. We're starting to put more and more textbooks into our schools. ... We've become accustomed of late of putting little books into the hands of children containing fables and moral lessons. ... We are spending less time in the classroom on the Bible, which should be the principal text in our schools. ... The Bible states these great moral lessons better than any other manmade book."[3]

The author of the First Amendment, in no uncertain terms, expressed his deep belief that the Bible should be the most important textbook in schools.

The author of the First Amendment, in no uncertain terms, expressed his deep belief that the Bible should be the most important textbook in schools. Not only that, but he warned that the replacement of the Bible with manmade fables was a "dangerous trend." Fisher Ames was right then, and he's still right over 230 years later. The most effective and most important education needs to be founded on biblical morals and values — that God is creator, we are His creation, and that all life is sacred.

If you were to walk around Washington D.C., you would see Bible verse after Bible verse, chiseled in stone in the halls of

---

3. https://www.biblia.work/sermons/amesfisher/.

the buildings and on the national monuments. America began as a nation founded by God's divine providence, with the Bible being the principal textbook in schools. Now, modern education focuses only on the negative aspects of our history, and disparages our Founding Fathers and founding documents. We've even gone so far as to pass laws restricting children from asking for a Bible in schools. Evolution has replaced creationism and instead of being created in the image of God, children are taught that they were created in the image of bacteria and monkeys. Imagine if our young people were taught that God Almighty loves them, and through His infinite wisdom, created them in His own image; and when He was finished creating them His response was, "It is good."

> "So then because thou art lukewarm, and neither cold
> nor hot, I will spue thee out of my mouth."
> — Revelation 3:16

Public schools are not just neutral on God, they're vehemently opposed to God. Multiple generations have now gone through a public school system that has, by law, removed God from education. (Remember the Indiana Supreme Court ruling on the Gideons in Indiana?) So what does God say about education?

> "He that is not with me is against me; and he that
> gathereth not with me scattereth abroad."
> — Matthew 12:30

A common misconception is that God is neutral on education, and that the Bible only focuses on morals, forgiveness, love, and faith. While those are themes throughout the Bible, God is not neutral on the topic of education. Education and the learning of concepts and skills are consistently present throughout the Old and New Testaments. For example, Noah built the Ark. Moses received the highest education available while living under Pharoah. Only the most-skilled craftsmen could've built the Tabernacle and Solomon's Temple. Jesus was called "Teacher" and learned carpentry from His dad. His disciples followed Him and received instruction while sitting at His feet. The five-fold ministry, given to the church by God, includes apostles, prophets, evangelists, pastors, and *teachers* (Ephesians 4:11). Matthew was a tax-collector. Paul was educated as a Pharisee and a Roman. God is the creator of mathematics, chemistry, physics, biology, and even the concept of time. None of this could be true without education, the processes of teaching and learning, having taken place.

So, if God is *not* neutral on education, it's fair to ask, "Then what *does* God say about education? What *is* the biblical approach to teaching and learning? What *should* be taught to our children?" One answer to these questions can be found in the New Testament:

> "His divine power has given to us all things that pertain to life and godliness, through the knowledge of Him who called us by glory and virtue." — 2 Peter 1:3; NKJV

Does God care about education? If it *pertains to life*, yes!

How does God address things that pertain to life? *Through knowledge.*

Through knowledge of what? *Knowledge of Him.*

So, if we want to learn something pertaining to this life, we must begin with learning about God. The Word of God is replete with instruction concerning this matter:

> "The fear of the LORD is the beginning of knowledge, but fools despise wisdom and instruction." — Proverbs 1:7; NKJV

> "Thy Word is a lamp unto my feet, and a light unto my path." — Psalms 119:105

> "Train up a child in the way he should go: and when he is old, he will not depart from it." — Proverbs 22:6

"Man shall not live by bread alone, but by every word that proceedeth out of the mouth of God." — Matthew 4:4

"Study to show thyself approved unto God, a workman that needeth not to be ashamed, rightly dividing the word of truth." — 2 Timothy 2:15

"My people are destroyed for lack of knowledge." — Hosea 4:6

"And even as they did not like to retain God in their knowledge, God gave them over to a reprobate mind." — Romans 1:28

"Blessed is the nation whose God is the LORD." — Psalms 33:12

The Christian approach to education can be summed up with this passage from the Old Testament:

"Love the LORD your God with all your heart and with all your soul and with all your strength. These commandments that I give you today are to be on your hearts. Impress them on your children. Talk about them when you sit at home and when you walk along the road, when you lie down and when you get up." Deuteronomy 6:5–7; NIV

God instructs parents to impress His commandments on the hearts of their children. To discuss them throughout the day, sitting at home, out in public, in the morning and at night. Parents are to be the first and primary educators in the life of a child. This is the biblical approach to education.

Parents are to be the first and primary educators in the life of a child.

7

School Boards and Teachers Unions

School boards and teachers unions are separate entities that often work closely with one another. School boards approve new hires, adopt new school curriculum, and oversee school funds and budgets. Teachers unions do things like bargain for contracts and safe working conditions. In short, the president runs the board, the board runs the school, the union runs the teachers, and the teachers run the classrooms.

❧ ❧

SCHOOL BOARDS

School board members, whether public or private, are either elected or appointed to those positions. Private school boards can be formed by regular elections or by self-replacement, which means the board itself (as opposed to a mayor) holds a vote to fill an empty seat. Private schools can offer more variety than public schools based on their constitutions and bylaws, which can determine how school boards are formed.

If the school board president is appointed, then the buck stops with whoever appointed them; in Chicago, for example, it's the mayor.

- 90% of school boards in America are *elected*
- 10% of school boards in America are *appointed* [1]

Let's take a quick look at CPS, Chicago, and the state of Illinois — since that's where I worked and experienced these trainings. The red flags and warning signs that are evident here may very well be evident in your local school district.

Every school district in the state of Illinois has an elected school board, except in the city of Chicago. Chicago Public Schools have never had an elected school board; instead, school board members have always been appointed by the mayor. Lori Lightfoot (D) was elected mayor of Chicago in 2019 and was the mayor while I taught for CPS during the 2020–2021 school year. Mayor Lori Lightfoot is responsible for the appointment of school board members and is ultimately responsible for the mandatory staff trainings that I was required to complete in 2020–2021, along with over 20,000 CPS teachers.[2] Mayor Lightfoot said in May of 2021 that she would no longer hold any interviews with white reporters but would only schedule meetings with black or brown reporters to "shine a spotlight on this most important issue."[3] This is clear racial discrimination on the part of Mayor Lightfoot and is being done in the name of racial equality. This logic is completely backwards. If this is the view of the mayor and the mayor appoints the school board members, it's no surprise that Chicago Public Schools are implementing Critical Race Theory and Gender Theory on a massive scale.

---

1. https://www.chicagotribune.com/news/ct-met-chicago-elected-school-board-debate-20190418-story.html.
2. https://www.chicagotribune.com/news/ct-met-chicago-elected-school-board-debate-20190418-story.html?outputType=amp.
3. https://nypost.com/2021/05/19/chicagos-mayor-refuses-to-give-interviews-to-white-reporters/).

In July of 2021, Illinois Governor J.B. Pritzker (D) signed a bill that will finally allow Chicagoans to vote and elect their own school board members — a process that will be phased in over several years. By 2024, there will be 11 members appointed by the mayor and 10 members elected by Chicagoans (the majority will still be appointed by the mayor); the school board will complete the transition and be entirely elected by 2026.[4]

CPS has 638 schools, 640,000+ students, and 38,000+ employees. Chicago makes up roughly 20% of the population of Illinois. Chicago Public Schools make up over 30% of the student population and over 20% of the teacher population in the entire state of Illinois; that means *at least* 1 in 3 of the children and 1 in 5 of the teachers in Illinois have been exposed to Marxist, socialist, communist ideologies.[5] And that's just one school corporation in one state. There are many more schools out there teaching the exact same stuff. In 2020–2021, Jefferson County Public Schools outside of Denver, Colorado, used the exact same Gender Unicorn training as CPS. It's as easy as point, click, share — just don't tell the parents.[6]

In America, our Founding Fathers intended for individual citizens to be the ruling class — kings and queens in our country — and our elected officials are there to represent us. When the people feel they're not being properly represented, they're provided opportunities to address their representatives. Unfortunately, it's become increasingly difficult and controversial for anyone, especially those with Christian values, to stand up in opposition to the progressive mob and social justice warriors who are so often supported by the public school boards. Parents' sacred duty does not stop at the school doors. It's way too late to assume your

---

4. https://chicago.chalkbeat.org/2021/7/30/22602068/illinois-governor-approves-elected-chicago-school-board.
5. https://www.cps.edu/about/stats-facts/.
6. (https://www.dailywire.com/news/colorado-school-district-instructs-teachers-to-avoid-informing-parents-if-their-child-shows-persistent-gender-confusion.

kid's school is immune from the impact of radical ideologies. Don't be passive with these things — be proactive! Stick to your values and stand up for your children! However, if you choose to take a stand against public schools, be ready for a battle. Below are just a few examples of the extreme push-back parents and teachers have recently received because they challenged the public school machine.

A 15-year-old was sexually assaulted by a male classmate in May of 2021 at Stone Bridge High School in Loudon County Virginia.[7] The male classmate identified as "gender fluid" and was wearing a skirt at the time of the assault, which took place in the girls' restroom. The girl's father was restrained and arrested outside a Loudon County School Board Meeting the following month after being involved in an argument with a

board member. The school board at the time claimed there was no record of any assault having taken place. Images were spread on national media of the father being handcuffed and dragged away from the board meeting while his pants were falling. Imagine  being the father: your daughter is sexually assaulted at school, in a girls' bathroom, during the school day and the school does nothing about it — in fact, they deny it and try to cover it up. Then, you're the one who is arrested, the national media slanders you, and you're labeled as a domestic terrorist — it's asinine. Welcome to the current state of public education!

On September 29, 2021, the National School Board Association cited the father's arrest in their letter to President Biden, which asked for assistance from the DOJ, FBI, U.S. Department of Homeland Security, U.S. Secret Service, and

---

7. https://www.dailywire.com/news/loudoun-school-board-was-informed-of-alleged-sexual-assault-the-day-it-happened-report.

the National Threat Assessment Center to put a stop to parents that commit, what they claim to be, "domestic terrorism and hate crimes" at school board meetings.[8] The NSBA claimed that threats, violence, and malice were coming from parents that were opposed to mask mandates, Gender Theory, and Critical Race Theory being taught in schools. The NSBA was adamant that CRT was not being taught in any K–12 schools in America — a statement that I know to be a flat-out lie, because I experienced mandatory teacher trainings on Gender Theory and CRT while I was a teacher for Chicago Public Schools during the 2020–2021 school year. There may not be textbooks or documentation or formal curriculum on the topics, but Gender Theory and CRT are all ingrained in America's public schools today. The National School Board Association, which represents over 90,000 school board members nationwide, was calling on the President of the United States to enlist the full power of the U.S. Government to go after upset parents at school board meetings.

Days after the NSBA wrote their letter to the President, Attorney General Merrick Garland issued his own statement in solidarity with the NSBA. In his statement, AG Garland expressed his own disapproval of concerned parents, noting that threats against public servants are illegal. It's ironic that these public servants, upon receiving negative feedback from the public they serve, respond by labeling the public as domestic terrorists and hate groups. Aren't the public servants accountable to the public? If the public is outraged at what the public servants are doing, the public servants are obligated to oblige the public, whom they serve and represent. The very opposite is happening here. These public servants are suppressing free speech and serving their own interests instead of the interests of their constituents. When parents tell school boards they don't want CRT in schools, but the school board

---

8. https://www.nsba.org/-/media/NSBA/File/nsba-letter-to-president-biden-concerning-threats-to-public-schools-and-school-board-members-92921.pdf?la=en&hash=642B7B91E0029BA4427D0F38D7054A007537160F.

doesn't listen, who exactly is making decisions on behalf of the students? Parental authority is effectively being removed and given over to the state. This is communism and it's being endorsed by the National School Board Association as well as the Attorney General of the United States.

As it turns out, simply claiming that something is a threat, act of violence, or act of intimidation doesn't make it true. Soon after their letter to the President, the NSBA issued an apology for calling parents "domestic terrorists." AG Garland even admitted in front of Congress that there has been no increase in violence at school board meetings. Unfortunately, the damage to reputations was already done well before any apologies were issued or context was given to situations. To reiterate a previous point, if you're a Christian and you plan on sending your children to public school, get ready for an inevitable and imminent conflict of values.

✺ ✺

TEACHERS UNIONS

The National Education Association (NEA) is the largest labor union in America with over three million members, including First Lady Jill Biden.[9] The American Federation of Teachers (AFT), whose President is Randi Weingarten, is the second-largest teachers union with nearly two million members.[10] Teachers unions are notoriously political and are heavily involved in political elections and activism. The two unions combined have been among the largest political donors since 1990, the majority of which support Democratic candidates.[11] The AFT, for example, endorsed Joe Biden for President in 2020 along with progressive policies like the Green New Deal.

---

9. https://www.nea.org/about-nea.
10. https://www.aft.org/join.
11. https://www.cato.org/commentary/teachers-unions-are-more-powerful-you-realize-may-be-changing#.

The NEA is a leftist group that votes on New Business Initiatives (NBI's) at their annual convention; NBI's are proposed national education policies. For example, at the 2022 convention one NBI called for a national policy on mandatory masking and Covid vaccines in schools. Another called for rejecting the words "mother" and "father" in exchange of "birthing person" and "non-birthing person." Another NBI included a child's "right to learn about and develop their own sexual orientation and gender identity."[12] This is completely inappropriate and borders on pedophilia.

In 2010, the NEA posted recommended reading on its website for any members interested in grassroots activism. The recommended readings were both books written by Saul Alinsky: *Reveille for Radicals* and *Rules for Radicals*.[13] Alinsky was a self-proclaimed radical and well-known American community activist. Hillary Clinton famously wrote her thesis on Alinsky, a role-model of hers. On the dedication page of his book *Rules for Radicals* Alinsky wrote:

> Lest we forget at least an over-the-shoulder acknowledgment to the very first radical: from all our legends, mythology, and history (and who is to know where mythology leaves off and history begins — or which is which), the first radical known to man who rebelled against the establishment and did it so effectively that he at least won his own kingdom — Lucifer.[14]

The NEA, which is the largest union in America, a union of teachers, openly endorsed the works of Alinsky — a man who openly was an admirer of Satan. If there was ever a reason to get out of public education, this is it! Alinsky's 13 rules for radicals to successfully implement societal change are:

---

12. https://www.dailywire.com/news/teachers-union-to-vote-on-mandatory-masking-enemies-list-rejecting-words-mother-and-father.

13. https://web.archive.org/web/20100823105309/http://www.nea.org/tools/17231.htm.

14. https://ia600309.us.archive.org/30/items/RulesForRadicals/RulesForRadicals.pdf.

1. Power is not only what you have but what the enemy thinks you have.
2. Never go outside the experience of your people.
3. Wherever possible go outside of the experience of the enemy.
4. Make the enemy live up to their own book of rules.
5. Ridicule is man's most potent weapon.
6. A good tactic is one that your people enjoy.
7. A tactic that drags on too long becomes a drag.
8. Keep the pressure on.
9. The threat is usually more terrifying than the thing itself.
10. Major premise for tactics is development of operations that will maintain constant pressure upon the opposition.
11. If you push a negative hard and deep enough it will break through into its counterside.
12. The price of a successful attack is a constructive alternative.
13. Pick the target, freeze it, personalize it, polarize it.

The NEA encouraged its members, the people who are teaching our nation's children every day in school, to read and apply these rules for radicals. I would like to address the NEA with a few follow-up questions, based on their recommended readings:

- Who exactly is the NEA's enemy?
- What is man's most potent weapon?
- Is ridicule something teachers are teaching children in school?
- Does the NEA support the use of threats and terrorizing people?
- If so, who are they threatening?
- What is the negative being pushed?
- How are you attacking?
- Who are you attacking?
- Who are your targets?

- How and why are you freezing them?
- Why are teachers personalizing and polarizing people?

The National Education Association has openly supported the Marxist ideals of tearing down systems, societal norms, and dividing society into two groups — oppressors vs. the oppressed. Millions of Teacher-Activists all over the country follow the NEA and impose these views in the classroom.

MY EXPERIENCE WITH TEACHERS UNIONS

I have never belonged to a teachers union, but I have had many interactions with them throughout my career. I have nothing against the idea of a union; my father was a union ironworker for nearly 30 years. He worked back-breaking jobs to provide for his family and I'd never shake my head at that. I do, however, have enormous problems with unions using member dues to support policies and initiatives that are anti-God, anti-America, and anti-truth.

I was in college during my first experience with a teachers union. In my hometown, the local school corporation had budget issues. As a result, they had to make cuts and let certain teachers go — starting with the Art, Music, and Physical Education teachers. When I finally became a teacher, I always remembered that P.E. was the first to go; the teachers union couldn't help them. So, why pay dues if you're the first on the chopping block?

My second union experience was tainted by the 2012 election. Political emails had been sent around, urging teachers to vote for one person or another and if we didn't, then our jobs would be in jeopardy. It was blackmail, basically — do this or else.

I did not join the Chicago Teachers Union (CTU) in my one year at Chicago Public Schools. CTU representatives reached out to me several times after I was hired (as is the custom with all new hires) asking if I would like to join CTU. It turned out that I was the only teacher in my school building that was not a union member. In fact, most teachers thought you automatically became a union member when you were hired. It wasn't really brought up, because not joining the union was so uncommon. However, my mind was made up because of what I learned about the Chicago Teachers Union after I was hired.

During the summer of 2020, cities across America were experiencing riots, looting, and absolute chaos. On August 27, 2020, Chicago Teachers Union tweeted an image of protesters gathered outside the home of Jeff Bezos, former CEO of Amazon. The protesters had constructed a guillotine outside the home of Bezos and were, apparently, threatening to decapitate him. Why? Bezos had just become the first individual in history to reach the mark of $200 billion in net worth. Chicago Teachers Union, one of the largest teacher groups in America, supported this action and tweeted that they were "impressed by and completely in support of wherever this was headed. #solidarity"

Let's unpack this. Jeff Bezos created a business, developed it for decades, now employs nearly a million people, and becomes incredibly wealthy as a result. One group's response to this news was to threaten to chop his head off outside of his home. That's bad. As bad as that is, the Chicago Teachers Union, which represents its 25,000+ members, joined in solidarity with this act. First of all, why is a teachers union focused on chopping off the head of a successful business owner? Shouldn't they be focused on teaching? Is that too much to ask? It makes you wonder what values and principles they're teaching to the 340,000+ students in the city's schools. Connect the dots — CTU tweets about beheading a billionaire and two months later CPS trains their staff that accumulating wealth is economically abusive.

Just weeks after that Twitter post, Chicago Public Schools resumed and began the year with virtual learning, as did most of the schools around the country. As weeks and months passed, more and more schools began to reopen. This was controversial because of the Covid hysteria. Was it safe to return or not? Was the risk worth going back to in-person learning? These were a few of the simple questions that reasonable people could disagree on. CTU's response to this national discussion came on December 6, 2020, in a Twitter post that stated:

> "The push to reopen schools is rooted in sexism, racism, and misogyny."

In two politically charged twitter posts, CTU threatened, ridiculed, and personalized their targets — tactics straight from the pages of Saul Alinsky's *Rules for Radicals*. CTU's message to parents was, if you want your kids to be in school amongst their peers, then you're sexist, racist, and misogynist. CTU's tweets were very much in-line with the "Intersecting Identities" training that all CPS teachers completed just a few weeks prior. Chicago Teachers Union and Chicago Public Schools are separate entities, often at odds with one another. However, here they marched in lockstep and they spoke the same language of wokeness, victimhood, division, prejudice, and discrimination. It's sad to say, but this clearly is not an example of a teachers union standing up for children. Instead, it's an example of the teachers union backing the ideologies being pushed by the school system.

In a way, CTU and CPS were quite successful — they talked the talk and walked the walk, using the plays straight from Saul Alinsky's Rules for Radicals playbook — name calling, labeling, division, threats, casting people as oppressor or oppressed — it's yet another example of Marxism in action.

The moral of the story is to be extremely involved in school board meetings, local elections, curriculum adoption, and the creation and implementation of school policy. Be the squeaky wheel or the neighbor that never stops knocking. If there's a board meeting — be there and have intentional questions ready to go. Get in line to speak and have it scripted out, rehearsed. If there's an issue at your child's school, set up a meeting with the principal. If there's a town hall meeting for your local elections, vet the candidates ten times more than you would the President of the United States. Better yet, run for local office yourself! Your mayor, school board members, and Chief of Police have real impacts on your daily life — just look at 2020 and what happened with quarantines, riots, looting, school closures, and mask mandates. Put the heat and pressure on your elected officials and hired administrators. Remember, your tax dollars run the local school system — these people work for you!

I tell you this because I've seen, first-hand, how destructive ideologies sneak in through the back door and creep into our public schools. I'm not a parent, but if I were I would be absolutely outraged to learn that my kindergartner was being shown graphic images and learning about sexual identity in their classroom — I was outraged as their teacher. I would be outraged to learn that my local school board teaches Critical Race Theory and Gender Theory — all without my prior knowledge or consent. I would be outraged to learn that my child's school teaches that the color of someone's skin, their gender, and their socioeconomic status predetermines their character. Thankfully, where public schools fail, homeschoolers can achieve great success.

8

Learning from Marxism and Communism in the 20th Century

The rise of communism, which is an atheist ideology, in the 20th century led to the death of over 100 million people worldwide; the education system was a key component everywhere that communism was implemented. Cleon Skousen was a former FBI agent who published an anti-communist book in 1958 titled *The Naked Communist*. Skousen explored the rise of communism around the world in a portion of his book called "Current Communist Goals." In this excerpt, he identified steps that had been taken to implement communism, and compiled a list of goals, or milestones, that would need to be achieved to instill communism in America. In 1963, the United States Congress issued this portion of Skousen's book into public record. The entire list is included below; nearly two-thirds of the goals directly impact education or require the use of schools as a means to implement communism (see those in italics).

1. U.S. acceptance of coexistence as the only alternative to atomic war.

2. U.S. willingness to capitulate in preference to engaging in atomic war.

3. Develop the illusion that total disarmament by the United States would be a demonstration of moral strength.

4. Permit free trade between all nations regardless of Communist affiliation and regardless of whether or not items could be used for war.

5. Extension of long-term loans to Russia and Soviet satellites.

6. Provide American aid to all nations regardless of Communist domination.

7. Grant recognition of Red China. Admission of Red China to the U.N.

8. Set up East and West Germany as separate states in spite of Khrushchev's promise in 1955 to settle the German question by free elections under supervision of the U.N.

9. Prolong the conferences to ban atomic tests because the United States has agreed to suspend tests as long as negotiations are in progress.

10. Allow all Soviet satellites individual representation in the U.N.

11. Promote the U.N. as the only hope for mankind. If its charter is rewritten, demand that it be set up as a one-world government with its own independent armed forces.

12. Resist any attempt to outlaw the Communist Party.

13. *Do away with all loyalty oaths.*

14. Continue giving Russia access to the U.S. Patent Office.

15. *Capture one or both of the political parties in the United States.*

16. *Use technical decisions of the courts to weaken basic American institutions by claiming their activities violate civil rights.*

17. *Get control of the schools. Use them as transmission belts for socialism and current Communist propaganda. Soften the curriculum. Get control of teachers' associations. Put the party line in textbooks.*
18. *Gain control of all student newspapers.*
19. *Use student riots to foment public protests against programs or organizations which are under Communist attack.*
20. *Infiltrate the press. Get control of book-review assignments, editorial writing, policymaking positions.*
21. *Gain control of key positions in radio, TV, and motion pictures.*
22. *Continue discrediting American culture by degrading all forms of artistic expression. An American Communist cell was told to "eliminate all good sculpture from parks and buildings, substitute shapeless, awkward and meaningless forms."*
23. *Control art critics and directors of art museums. "Our plan is to promote ugliness, repulsive, meaningless art."*
24. *Eliminate all laws governing obscenity by calling them "censorship" and a violation of free speech and free press.*
25. *Break down cultural standards of morality by promoting pornography and obscenity in books, magazines, motion pictures, radio, and TV.*
26. *Present homosexuality, degeneracy, and promiscuity as "normal, natural, healthy."*
27. *Infiltrate the churches and replace revealed religion with "social" religion. Discredit the Bible and emphasize the need for intellectual maturity which does not need a "religious crutch."*
28. *Eliminate prayer or any phase of religious expression in the schools on the ground that it violates the principle of "separation of church and state."*
29. *Discredit the American Constitution by calling it inadequate, old-fashioned, out of step with modern needs, a hindrance to cooperation between nations on a worldwide basis.*

30. *Discredit the American Founding Fathers. Present them as selfish aristocrats who had no concern for the "common man."*

31. *Belittle all forms of American culture and discourage the teaching of American history on the ground that it was only a minor part of the "big picture." Give more emphasis to Russian history since the Communists took over.*

32. *Support any socialist movement to give centralized control over any part of the culture — education, social agencies, welfare programs, mental health clinics, etc.*

33. *Eliminate all laws or procedures which interfere with the operation of the Communist apparatus.*

34. Eliminate the House Committee on Un-American Activities.

35. Discredit and eventually dismantle the FBI.

36. *Infiltrate and gain control of more unions.*

37. *Infiltrate and gain control of big business.*

38. *Transfer some of the powers of arrest from the police to social agencies. Treat all behavioral problems as psychiatric disorders which no one but psychiatrists can understand or treat.*

39. *Dominate the psychiatric profession and use mental health laws as a means of gaining coercive control over those who oppose Communist goals.*

40. *Discredit the family as an institution. Encourage promiscuity and easy divorce.*

41. *Emphasize the need to raise children away from the negative influence of parents. Attribute prejudices, mental blocks and retarding of children to suppressive influence of parents.*

42. *Create the impression that violence and insurrection are legitimate aspects of the American tradition; that students and special-interest groups should rise up and use "united force" to solve economic, political or social problems.*

43. Overthrow all colonial governments before native populations are ready for self-government.

44. Internationalize the Panama Canal.

45. Repeal the Connally reservation so the United States cannot prevent the World Court from seizing jurisdiction over domestic problems. Give the World Court jurisdiction over nations and individuals alike.[1]

An education not founded on the belief in God quickly devolves into a dangerous education, as evidenced by the above list of communist goals. After reading through this list once, it's clear to see: 1) the importance of education, 2) nearly all of the communist goals have already been achieved in America, and 3) the urgency with which America must return to teaching biblical morality, love of God, love of country, and traditional family values. Dr. Ben Carson stated, "*The Naked Communist* lays out the whole progressive plan. It is unbelievable how fast it has been achieved."[2] President Ronald Reagan said about Skousen and his book, "No one is better qualified to discuss the threat to this nation from communism. You will be alarmed, you will be informed, and you'll be glad you heard him."[3]

The following individuals led regimes that were responsible for approximately 100 million deaths during the 20th century. Each implemented Marxist/socialist/communist ideologies using education, propaganda, and government force.

Vladimir Lenin
- Marxist/Socialist/Communist leader during the founding of the USSR (1917–1924)
- Responsible for deaths of approximately 5 million due to famine, execution, and civil war[4]

Joseph Stalin
- Leader of the Stalinist (Socialist/Communist) Soviet Union (1927–1953)

1. http://www.ecjones.org/1963_Communist_Goals.pdf.
2. https://www.audible.com/pd/The-Naked-Communist-Audiobook/B017XXEUGQ.
3. https://wcleonskousen.com/books/the-naked-communist/.
4. https://www.history.com/topics/russia/vladimir-lenin.

- Responsible for deaths of 20–40 million due to forced labor, famine, disease, gulags, and mass executions[5][6]

Adolf Hitler
- Leader of the Nazi Party (National Socialist) during the Holocaust (1933–1945)
- Responsible for deaths of 6 million Jews due to forced relocation, famine, disease, and mass executions carried out by the Nazi regime[7]

Mao Zedung
- Chairman of the Chinese Communist Party (Marxist/Communist) (1935–1976)
- Responsible for deaths of up to 65 million Chinese people because of execution, famine, or imprisonment[8]

Pol Pot
- Leader of the Cambodian Communist Party (1975–1979)
- Modeled after Mao Zedung's Chinese Communist Party
- Responsible for deaths of 2 million Cambodians (approximately 1/4 of the population) in the Cambodian Genocide because of forced labor, mass executions, famine, and disease[9]

Kim il-sung (1948–1994), **Kim Jong-il** (1994–2011) and **Kim Jong-un** (2011–present)
- Family dynasty that has controlled North Korea since World War 2

5. https://www.history.com/topics/russia/joseph-stalin.
6. https://www.dailymail.co.uk/home/moslive/article-2091670/Hitler-Stalin-The-murderous-regimes-world.html.
7. https://www.history.com/topics/world-war-ii/adolf-hitler-1.
8. heritage.org.
9. https://www.history.com/topics/cold-war/pol-pot.

- Totalitarian regime that implements Marxist/Socialist/Communist ideologies
- Currently running concentration camps, prison camps, and labor camps
- Currently have nuclear weapons

The purpose of the next few sections is to highlight the ways that the education system was used during the 20th century by ruthless and murderous dictators, to learn from it, and to avoid ever repeating the same mistakes.

USSR/SOVIET UNION

Education in Soviet/Communist Russia

Nigel Grant was born in 1932 and later became a professor at the University of Glasgow. He said that Soviet education was, "An instrument of mass education from which the younger generation gain not only their formal learning, but their social, moral and political ideas as well."[10] Vladimir Lenin, the Soviet leader when the USSR was founded, was very intentional on politicizing education in the USSR. Regarding the illiteracy problem, he stated, "As long as there is such a thing in the country as illiteracy it is hard to talk about political education."[11] He also said about education, "Without teaching there is no knowledge and without knowledge there is no communism."[12] Lenin also said that kindergarten and nurseries were "the sprouts of Communism."[13]

Between 1914 and 1939, Russia made the following efforts to speed up and solidify the development of communism:

---

10. Nigel Grant, *Soviet Education* (London, England: Penguin Books, 1970).
11. Ben Eklof, *Russian Literacy Campaigns* (Boston, MA: Springer), p. 134.
12. https://stalinsocietygb.wordpress.com/2017/01/19/education-in-the-soviet-union/.
13. https://www.rbth.com/history/328721-education-in-ussr-the-best.

- Approximately 73% of the population was illiterate and only about 25% of all children ever attended school in pre-Soviet Russia.[14]
- The number of children in full-time education increased from 8 million in 1914 to 47 million by 1939.
- Attendance in secondary schools increased from 1 million in 1914 to over 12 million by 1939.
- The number of university students increased from 112,000 in 1914 to 601,000 by 1939.
- More schools were built in 20 years in the USSR than in the previous 200 years combined.

Reading, writing, and arithmetic, also known as the "Three R's of education," were not highly esteemed in the USSR. Competencies in reading, measuring, and writing were seen as limiting a person's full potential. The Three R's were viewed as rote and mindless propaganda, used to enslave an educated population by restricting their knowledge to a tiny box. In contrast, the Soviet style of education claimed to teach the truth about nature and society and empowered students to face complex situations in society; it would lead students to expand their understanding and experience true freedom.[15]

Revisionism is a process that occurs over time and effectively changes the history of a nation. Revisionism, especially in education, is commonly earmarked by the removal of old texts and the adoption of new texts. Revisionism in the Soviet Union began when Lenin's Bolshevik/Communist Party took power in 1917 because of the Bolshevik Revolution, which

> *Revisionism is a process that occurs over time and effectively changes the history of a nation.*

---

14. https://stalinsocietygb.wordpress.com/2017/01/19/education-in-the-soviet-union/.
15. https://www.dailymail.co.uk/home/moslive/article-2091670/Hitler-Stalin-The-murderous-regimes-world.html.

proved to be a major victory in Lenin's goal of making the USSR a communist nation. The Soviet educational system replaced traditional education (mathematics, reading, writing) with a more sociological education, focused on collectivism and how students would contribute to society after their schooling was complete. In Communist Russia, traditional education was seen as outdated and obsolete, something students couldn't relate to anymore, which supported the revisionist process of replacing historical or traditional texts with new, more progressive texts.[16]

Teachers that were effective in teaching the Soviet style of education were praised, honored, and rewarded. Teachers that were not "successful" were criticized and most often eliminated from their profession. The Soviet standard of education was set and if a teacher did not meet the standard, they were phased out. Over time, only the "good" teachers would remain.[17]

Students often played prominent roles in Soviet classrooms and were almost seen as equals with the teacher. Because they were given much responsibility, they also had much pull in classes. If a teacher was not up to snuff, the students could influence whether that teacher kept their job. The culture was such that if a student failed academically, then instead of blaming themselves, they could blame their teacher's methodology. This is a Marxist ideal which states that a child is the product of their environment, and it takes a village to raise a child. Consequently, it takes responsibility off the individual and places it on the group — individuality is not encouraged, but collectivism is. Whatever is best for the group is what's done, no matter what your personal talents, opinions, goals, or beliefs may be. Students all followed the same curriculum, meaning that a high-achieving student would use their spare time helping students who work slower. This sounds nice,

16. Anna-Louise Strong, *The First Time in History*, chapter 11, "Education in Soviet Russia" (New York: Boni & Liveright, 1922), www.marxists.org.

17. Deana Levin, *Children in Soviet Russia* (London: Faber & Faber Ltd., 1942).

but in reality it restricts high achievers by forcing them to sacrifice their own education for the good of the whole. This is conditioning for a communist society.

Parents typically were highly involved in schooling. They were encouraged to frequent the schools and even visit the classrooms. Teachers commonly visited students at home to better understand any problems that might be occurring. It was common for schools (not the parents) to dictate what children were and were not able to do. For example, schools commonly had school governments which would make all the decisions for the school. Things like how to spend funds, what food to grow in the school garden, and what subjects should be taught.[18]

These are the seeds of communism being normalized through education. The government takes from the group and decides how to distribute the resources; individuals do the work, but don't get to choose how to spend their own money. It's a path that throughout history has proven to lead to corruption of the worst kind.

⊘⬿ ⬿⊘

GERMANY

Pre-Nazi Germany

Prior to 1933, there was an unemployment crisis in Germany. As many as six million Germans were unemployed leading up to Hitler's regime.

> *Germany was mostly a Christian nation prior to 1933, with as many as 45 million Protestants and 22 million Catholics.*

Germany was mostly a Christian nation prior to 1933, with as many as 45 million Protestants and 22 million Catholics.

18. https://isreview.org/issue/82/education-literacy-and-russian-revolution/index.html.

Post-Nazi Germany

Part of the Nazi campaign promised to fix the unemployment problem and, by 1938, the Nazi party claimed that unemployment had fallen to zero — it seemed they'd fixed unemployment. In 1933, the Nazi party banned trade unions, arrested their leaders, and took control of workers' rights such as hours of work and rate of pay; the Nazi government controlled it all. Through this process, citizens would work, but only as the government stipulated, and would receive small rewards such as theater tickets. The idea was to create a happy, though powerless, working class while the Nazi party became more powerful. One example of the slow growth of government control was the building of the German Motorway, also known as the Autobahn. This building project recruited young, unskilled men ages 18–25. However, by 1935 the work became mandatory for men as part of a rearmament initiative — the government required men to do the work as a military need, regardless of their personal preference.

While the unemployment numbers in Nazi Germany did drop, so did hourly rates, working conditions, worker safety, and personal freedom. One thing that did go up, however, was the number of hours worked per week; the average work week grew to 60–72 hours. The unemployment numbers did not factor in political prisoners and those who were forced out of work, such as Jewish teachers and non-Nazi sympathizers.

Like the trade unions, religion threatened the power of the Nazi party. Given that most Germans were either Protestant or Catholic Christians, it was not easy for the Nazi regime to impose their conflicting ideology on such a religious population. In 1933 the Nazi party signed an agreement with the Vatican to gain legitimacy. Soon after, in 1935, the Nazis broke the contract and established the Ministry for Church Affairs which undermined religion and enacted anti-religious policies. Simultaneously, the Reich Church was established to create a new national church that was favorable toward

Nazism. In these Reich Churches, the Old Testament was not allowed to be taught as it was considered a Jewish document. Preachers, pastors, priests, and church leaders who fought against the Nazi regime were removed, imprisoned, or placed in concentration camps.

Education in Nazi Germany between 1933 and 1945 saw the establishment of three different types of schools: *Napolas, Adolph Hitler Schools,* and *Order Castles.* All these new types of schools existed solely to educate future Nazi politicians and party leaders.

Revisionism in Germany was like revisionism in the USSR — indoctrination began in schools with the removal of texts, adoption of new texts, and changing of the curriculum — all of which was first approved by the Nazi party. Under the rule of Hitler, schools in Nazi Germany replaced traditional education with sports, new history, and racial science. New concepts began to be taught, such as "Lebensraum," which promulgates the need and right of Germans, or German-speaking people, to own more land. By 1938, German students were studying sports as much as five hours a day; the subject of religion was removed altogether.[19]

Hitler held five basic principles concerning the use of propaganda:

- Avoid abstract ideas — appeal to the emotions.
- Constantly repeat just a few ideas. Use stereotyped phrases.
- Give only one side of the argument.
- Continuously criticize your opponents.
- Pick out one special "enemy" for special vilification.[20]

---

19. https://www.theholocaustexplained.org/life-in-nazi-occupied-europe/controlling-everyday-life/controlling-education/.
20. Garth Jowett and Victoria O'Donnell, *Propagation and Persuasion* (Thousand Oaks, CA: Sage Publications).

Teachers were subject to intense scrutiny. The Restoration of the Professional Civil Service Act of April 7, 1933 (three months after Hitler became Chancellor of Germany), allowed for the removal of all Jewish teachers, including university professors, and teachers who were not supporters of the Nazi party. Furthermore, membership in the Nazi party became a prerequisite to become a teacher. The National Socialist Teachers League required Germany's teachers to attend a one-month long training course where they were taught the Nazi ideology and how to effectively implement it in their classrooms. If you weren't a Nazi then you couldn't be a teacher, it's that simple.

Students were subject to the Nazi indoctrination process. Sports became a large part of the school day and students were taught that the German race was superior to others, especially compared to the Jews. By 1938, all Jewish students were banned from attending public schools or universities in Germany.

Parents were subject to the intense and relentless propaganda machine of Joseph Goebbels, Hitler's Minister of Propaganda, with the intent that they would reinforce the Nazi indoctrination that their children were learning at school. Joseph Goebbels had been a member of the Nazi party since 1924 and was, arguably, the main protagonist of the Holocaust. In 1945, after Hitler's eventual suicide, Goebbels became Chancellor of Germany for a short time. He and his wife would go on to poison and kill their six children before they both committed suicide.

Goebbels used virtually every medium to push Nazi propaganda — art, music, literature, and entertainment to name a few. Old or historical art was removed and replaced with new and "better" art. Jewish authors were blacklisted along with anyone considered an enemy of the Nazi party — a process that led to the infamous socialist/fascist "book burnings" led by the National Socialist German Student Association.

Keeping with the Nazi theme, music was also reserved only for Nazi sympathizers. Genres such as jazz or swing music were banned, along with anything from the Jewish community, of course. Theaters and newspapers were also used by Goebbels to indoctrinate the population. Anti-Semitic images, headlines, and stories were commonplace in Nazi culture — further implanting the hatred and racism toward the Jewish people.

≈ ≈

CHINA

Pre-Communist China

The Nationalist Party was one of the dominant political parties in China during the early 20th century, before Mao's reign as head of the Chinese Communist Party (CCP). While China was Communist during the early 1900s, it was not totalitarian or dictatorial until Mao came to power in 1949. The Nationalist Party came to power through a series of revolutions against the former Chinese Monarchy and were aided by Vladimir Lenin and the Soviets. Mao Zedung, who would eventually rise to power as the head of the Chinese Communist Party (CCP), was once the head of the Propaganda Department in the Chinese Nationalist Party; Joseph Goebbels held a similar office, Minister of Propaganda, in Hitler's Nazi regime.[21]

Post-Communist China

Mao Zedung came to power in 1949 and was faced with much opposition within his own country. The Chinese Communist Party was not supported by all of China's citizens, including capitalist businessmen, Christians, and the weakened Nationalist Party.[22] Similar to Hitler and Stalin, Mao used a variety of tactics to suppress his perceived political enemies.

21. https://www.britannica.com/biography/Mao-Zedong/Mao-and-the-Chinese-Communist-Party#ref12451.
22. https://alphahistory.com/chineserevolution/dealing-with-opposition/.

Revisionism in China ramped up in the 1940s and 1950s and lasted until Mao's death in 1976. The Suppression of Counter Revolutionaries campaign was established in March of 1950, less than a year after Mao came to power, and helped launch Mao's communist takeover. The goal of this campaign, among several other similar movements, was to identify those who opposed Mao's CCP and to label them as Revolutionaries, or enemies. Mao acknowledged the need for skilled laborers and successful businessmen, thus he decided to use propaganda instead of coercion to suppress any political opposition — Mao's previous experience as head of propaganda for the Nationalist Party would prove to serve him well. Any person, party, or idea that opposed Mao's CCP would be demonized, discredited, cast as a villain, and done away with completely. Many leaders of religious groups, such as Christian Churches and Buddhist Temples, were exiled, imprisoned, or executed simply for existing in communist China. The Suppression of Counter Revolutionaries campaign reached a fever pitch in 1951 when large public meetings were held in a stadium or arena. Individuals that were labeled as revolutionaries, enemies, or suspects were marched on stage, presented to the large crowds, identified, intimidated, and embarrassed. For such individuals, their careers would be threatened, along with their businesses, jobs, and even their very lives. This identification and demonizing process led to the execution of up to 700,000 people under Mao's murderous rule.

After nearly a decade of rule, Mao implemented The Great Leap Forward program in 1958. This program held an ambitious goal of increasing labor production, particularly in industry and agriculture. This plan eventually failed and would lead to mass famine and death in communist China.[23] After a failed program and weakened reputation, Mao launched the Cultural Revolution in 1966 in an attempt to revive the revolution spirit and stomp out any ideologies that were contrary to Mao's Marxist/communist beliefs.

---

23. https://www.bbc.co.uk/history/historic_figures/mao_zedong.shtml.

From Mao's perspective, if you were useful to him or the CCP, then he would control you through propaganda. If you were not useful or supportive of the CCP, then you were exiled, imprisoned, or executed. Like Hitler's Nazi Germany and Stalin's communist Russia, Mao's communist China used propaganda to spread lies, used fear to intimidate, and used coercion or murder to remove those who disagreed.

Like Hitler's Nazi Germany and Stalin's communist Russia, Mao's communist China used propaganda to spread lies, used fear to intimidate, and used coercion or murder to remove those who disagreed.

Education was an important weapon for Mao, who wrote that literature and art "operate as powerful weapons for uniting and educating the people and for attacking and destroying the enemy."[24] Much of China's peasant population was illiterate leading up to Mao's reign, so the CCP propaganda machine would use simple art prints, posters, banners, and other images to win people over. In these images, Mao and CCP leaders were made to look honest, attractive, smart, pious, and almost God-like. This would allow citizens, educated and illiterate, to view the CCP in a positive light and be more willing to comply with CCP policies and demands.[25] China followed the Soviet model of education in the early 1950s and placed an emphasis on science and technology.

The Great Leap Forward also marked a shift in educational priorities; now there was a new emphasis on politics and class background.[26] The state-run school system identified certain schools as "key" schools, which would receive the best teachers, students, training, and equipment available.

24. Powell, Patricia and Joseph Wong, "Propaganda Posters from the Chinese Cultural Revolution," *The Historian*, 2007: 777–793.
25. Stefan R. Landsberger, "Mao as the Kitchen God: Religious Aspects of the Mao Cult During the Cultural Revolution," *China Information*, 1996: 196–211.
26. William G. Saywell, "Education in China Since Mao," *The Canadian Journal of Higher Education*, 1980, https://files.eric.ed.gov/fulltext/EJ228175.pdf.

To begin separating itself from the Soviet Union, Mao instituted a new initiative in 1967 called The Great Proletarian Cultural Revolution. This new policy insisted that curriculum in China's schools and universities be completely changed. As a result, educational facilities at all levels were suspended until this new curriculum could be developed and implemented.

Teachers were phased out during the school closures. After the school closures of 1967–68, educational facilities began to reopen in China in late 1968 and into the early 1970s. Mao's propaganda teams took to universities to prepare for the return of teachers and students. Instituting the new curriculum was not seamless, and teachers and administrators who were not compliant were removed. New teacher training was emphasized along with condensing and simplifying curriculum, which trended toward student activism and politics. Teachers that were not politically aligned with Mao were replaced, frequently by inexperienced workers and peasants. The quality of the teacher was not important, rather the politics of the teacher.

Students, because of Mao's various policies, were often engaged in a work-study program, which was a program rooted in Chinese communism. In addition to providing labor as a prerequisite, class background and "ideological purity" were also criteria for admission. During the school closures of the late 1960s to early 1970s, many students were forced by the Chinese Red Guard to do their manual labor, which was required for admission to university, only now there was no hope of the promised education. Mao's policy promised education in exchange for manual labor, but once the manual labor was provided, the promise of education was removed. This forced labor often led to the student-workers being murdered or committing suicide, contributing to the death toll of Mao's regime.

For younger students, education for all was preferred above a better education for the highly qualified; this education system stressed student activism and political studies. Academics were not as relevant as politics and student failure was almost obsolete, not because of academic achievement, but because of lowered standards.

Universities began to reopen in the 1970s and the admission requirements were changed. The new criteria were physical fitness, academic achievement, and political awareness. An applicant's coworkers voted on whether they were deserving to be admitted. If an applicant's political affiliation was not favorable, the coworkers were obligated to vote against the applicant. The next step would be for the application to move on to an evaluation committee, which served as a safeguard against any revolutionaries and was highly corruptible, placing preference upon family members and political allies. The emphasis was not on academics, but on political affiliation, class, and knowing the right people.

Parents and families, from Mao's perspective, were seen as oppressive toward peasants. Mao was born into the peasant class and was determined to break down the family unit — at least the parts that he labeled as oppressive. Mao became a Marxist as a young adult and founded the Chinese Communist party in 1921. Basic Marxism teaches that one group (peasants) is oppressed, and the other group (families) is the oppressor. Mao held a Marxist view (oppressor vs. oppressed) toward families and the peasant class. Once Mao came to power in 1949, he began his attempt to dismantle the family by not allowing houses to have kitchens, thus forcing families to eat in cafeterias. In addition, more children were raised in daycares instead of by family and relatives. Even further, family records and ancestries were destroyed.[27]

With the rise of communism came the rise in labor and forced labor. More women began to work, which was a big cultural shift for traditional Chinese families. Divorce became more common and many factories provided childcare

27. https://chinachange.org/2011/03/17/the-chinese-family-under-mao/.

services, which contributed toward Mao's attempt to weaken the family structure.

꿍 꿍

CAMBODIA

Revisionism began in Cambodia when Lon Nol was the president from 1970 to 1975, before Pol Pot and the Communist Party of Cambodia (Kampuchea), also known as the Khmer Rouge, led a rebellion to remove him from power. Lon Nol was marked for execution by the Khmer Rouge and he resigned from his position in 1975, at which point Pol Pot assumed power.[28]

Pol Pot, a Marxist-Leninist and admirer of Mao Zedung, is largely responsible for the Cambodian Genocide, which claimed nearly two million lives between 1975 and 1979; starvation, execution, disease, and slave labor were the most common causes of death during this span. The Communist Party of Kampuchea (Cambodia), also known as the Khmer Rouge, ruled Cambodia during this time span.

The Khmer Rouge was known for targeting groups of people that may not have supported them politically. These people were labeled as "new people" and often included Buddhist monks, ethnic minorities, and educated elites.[29] The "new people" were not part of the revolution against the Lon Nol regime and, as a result, were considered untrustworthy and suspect. Often, when rice production was down and people were going hungry, the Khmer Rouge blamed the "new people" and capitalism. Because these "new people" were constantly blamed and considered to be traitors, they began to hide their identity and try to blend in.

---

28. https://www.globalsecurity.org/military/world/cambodia/history-lon-nol.htm.
29. Chigas, George & Mosyakov, Dmitri, *Literacy and Education Under the Khmer Rouge* (https://gsp.yale.edu/literacy-and-education-under-khmer-rouge.

Teachers in Cambodia experienced the process of removal and replacement. Erasing or altering the history of a nation is a major step in establishing a revolution; the Khmer Rouge was determined to erase parts of Cambodia's history that were not favorable to communism. To accomplish this goal, past political parties, officials, and rulers were labeled as oppressors, making them much easier to remove from society, schools, and textbooks — this, of course, extended to teachers and professors. Individualism and independent thought were discouraged by the Khmer Rouge, because independent thinkers were harder to control. If a person was concerned about individual benefits, there would be no reason to comply with the Khmer Rouge, because there was virtually no individual reward for labor. Teachers that could convince students to promote communism were more valuable than teachers that were highly qualified in a particular subject area.[30] Politics were prioritized above academics. Propaganda over truth. Fear and compliance over freedom.

> *Individualism and independent thought were discouraged by the Khmer Rouge, because independent thinkers were harder to control.*

Students, particularly highly educated individuals, were often considered suspect by the Khmer Rouge, but that doesn't mean Pol Pot's communist regime was against education — they were simply against not being in control of education. Education was so important to the Khmer Rouge that they issued three publications each month. Young students were often required to keep detailed notebooks in which all the communist propaganda would be kept, along with information about their families, hobbies, and political leanings.[31] Marxism requires an educated and literate population that can read and understand whatever the government wants

---

30. Ibid.
31. Ibid.

them to read and understand — revolutions and culture shifts are much easier this way. A Marxist-communist government wants its people to read and write, but they want to control what the people read and write. Education wasn't the problem in communist Cambodia, so long as it was favorable to the Khmer Rouge, Pol Pot, and communism.

Students were taught the "correct way" to read, meaning don't question what you read — just read it and accept it. No critical thought, no questions, just compliance. Any student that would question a source or ideology would be labeled as a traitor and corrupt. The use of propaganda was ramped up over time as the independent thinkers were rooted out — with the traitors gone, the rest of the population was easy to control. **Parents** and families saw their role in Cambodian society begin to decline as the Khmer Rouge relocated people from cities to the countryside to work in fields. The mismanagement of the government would lead to food shortages, disease, famine, and mass death. As a result, more children were raised without parents and were left to the mercies of communism.[32]

NORTH KOREA

Marxist/socialist/communist ideologies control North Korea and have for three generations under the Kim family. North Korea uses propaganda, fear, coercion, and total government control to implement communist rule, just like the past regimes of Soviet Russia, Nazi Germany, communist China, and communist Cambodia. Human rights violations are taking place right now in North Korea (2022). These horrors are as bad, or worse, than the atrocities carried out by Lenin, Stalin, Hitler, Mao, and Pol Pot. Supreme Leader Kim Jong-un, with the help of the Worker's Party of Korea (WPK) are overseeing

---

32. University of Minnesota, College of Liberal Arts: Holocaust and Genocide Studies. (https://cla.umn.edu/chgs/holocaust-genocide-education/resource-guides.

famine, starvation, concentration camps, prison camps, labor camps, executions, and horrific living conditions in North Korea. These are major crimes against humanity, and they are all too common in North Korea. Marxist/socialist/communist ideologies are to blame.

Revisionism in North Korea is absolute, meaning that North Korea's history starts with the Kim family; anything that existed before their reign is effectively erased from society. When Kim il-sung came to power after World War 2, he ordered background checks on all citizens. He wanted to find out just how loyal everyone would be to his regime. He divided citizens into three groups based on his perception of their loyalty: core, basic, and hostile.[33] The core group were friends of the Kim family. The basic group consisted of workers, intellectuals, and those considered loyal to the Kims. The hostile group consisted of landowners and their families, Christians, other religious groups, and families of political enemies. This is a Marxist principle of labeling and dividing society into groups that are against each other.

In North Korea, the God of the Bible has been replaced with Kim Jong-il, and Jesus has been replaced with Kim Jong-un. They make themselves deity. They make themselves gods. As such, nobody has the authority to question or defy them. They'll know if you ever think about defying them, because North Koreans are taught that the Supreme Leader can read minds. Every home in North Korea must have a photo of Kim Jong-un hanging on the wall, and dust on the photo is reason enough for execution. There is one news channel in North Korea that controls information, or propaganda, given to citizens. Nazi Germany used a similar tactic to hide the mass murder that was taking place in their concentration camps, by forcing prisoners to write letters to family members saying how wonderful the camps were. All forms of communication within the Nazi concentration camps — letters, photos, news-

---

33. Yeonmi Park, *In Order to Live* (New York: Penguin Press, 2015).

papers — were screened. North Korea uses the same tactics. Only favorable propaganda is permitted. This total censorship is meant to keep both the citizens and the outside world ignorant of the evil truth.

Teachers in North Korea are subject to regular trainings that are aligned with the communist policies of the Worker's Party of Korea. Teachers are required to meet with propaganda officers every week to be trained on the current political policies being implemented by the WPK. Teachers are then expected to implement the WPK policies in their classrooms and pass the ideologies down to the children.[34] The Communist ideals of the WPK are integrated into all subject areas. For example, word problems in math are phrased in such a way as to paint America or capitalism as evil.

Students are conditioned to support the political policies and positions of the supreme leader of North Korea. Teachers simply pass down the propaganda they receive from the government, and students are taught to support the agenda of the Kim regime. There is no free press or media, so every book, magazine, picture, and piece of news is propaganda. Students receive only the information that the government allows them to receive and has created for them. Students are read stories that portray Kim il-sung, Kim Jong-il, and Kim Jong-un as brave, heroic, moral characters worthy of admiration.[35] Students are made to believe that North Korea is the greatest place on earth and that everyone wants to get into North Korea, even though most North Koreans live in extreme poverty and are malnourished.[36]

Parents have little freedom to instill values into their children. Language and words are heavily censored in North Korea, so parents can't pass on values like "love" and "liberty," because those words don't exist in North Korea — the only affection

---

34. http://pscore.org/life-north-korea/forced-to-hate/.
35. Ibid.
36. Yeonmi Park, *In Order to Live* (New York: Penguin Press, 2015).

or sentiment one can feel is toward the Kim family.[37] There is no private property in North Korea; everything is owned by the government. It is common for homes to go without electricity for weeks, even months at a time. Prior to the end of the Cold War, communist countries like the Soviet Union and China had been helping support North Korea by providing basic needs to citizens — food, clothes, and medicine. Under Kim il-sung's rule, North Korea had been a Marxist/communist country, meaning the state owned everything. All farms were owned by the state. All homes and jobs were provided by the state. Anything and everything produced was controlled by the state and if anyone attempted to make a private product or profit on the black market, they would be killed. After the Cold War, that support dwindled, and North Koreans were on their own. Under Kim Jong-il, neighborhoods were divided into units where the people were instructed to inform on any neighbor who spoke against the regime. Violators could be taken away and placed in prison camps, often never to be seen again.

LEARNING FROM HISTORY

This particular history teaches us that:

1. Values matter
2. Ideologies matter
3. Governments are capable of horrific things when given too much power and control
4. Propaganda and education are extremely powerful
5. The sanctity of the family unit is immensely important

These themes were center stage in Stalin's Marxist/communist Soviet Union, Hitler's Nazi Germany, Mao's communist China, Pol Pot's communist Cambodia, and the Kim regimes in North Korea. The ideologies of Marxism, socialism, and communism

---

37. Ibid.

lead to authoritarianism, totalitarianism, and dictatorships. They are atheist ideologies that thirst for control and use citizens as a means to an end. Governments throughout history, especially these five regimes, have consistently proved to be incompetent at best and evil at worst. Myriads of failed policies, coupled with overwhelming control over the population is a recipe for disaster — as evidenced by the nearly 100 million people that died as a result of communism in the 20th century.

Each regime held similar ideologies. Each regime, through total and corrupt government control, was responsible for killing their own citizens. Each regime heavily relied on propaganda and used the school systems to indoctrinate the youth. Finally, each regime destroyed families through physical relocation, ideological indoctrination and separation, forced labor, state-sponsored childcare, or execution. When the government actively divides its citizens and casts one group as oppressed and the other as the oppressor, the nation is in danger. When the government responds to a crisis by creating radical policy — which will only lead to further crisis and an even more radical policy — the nation is in danger. When the government promises you safety and security in exchange for your freedom, the nation is in danger.

Each of these governments took measures to remove dissenters, independent thinkers, and political enemies from society, either by publicly shaming them, removing them from work, firing them, imprisoning them, forcing them to do labor, relocating them, or by executing them. These Marxist/communist governments would first label those that did not support their ideology as suspect, threats, enemies, thieves, rats, or revolutionaries who were responsible for the woes of society and failings of the government. Then, once the labels were in place and division was established, the government would create a new policy or initiative that would systematically remove the troublemakers and have them replaced with ideological supporters. When the government silences people who think differently, the nation is in danger. When the government labels its own citizens as threats, the nation is in danger. When the government creates policies that target law-abiding citizens, the nation is in danger.

Education is so powerful that corrupt governments have used it to accomplish horrible things on a massive scale. The act of pitting one group against another through propaganda and indoctrination — effectively dismantling houses, families, communities, and nations — is a Marxist tactic that was employed by Stalin, Hitler, Mao, Pol Pot, and the Kims. Children vs. parents, students vs. teachers, citizen vs. citizen, old vs. new, God vs. government; these are hallmarks of every Marxist/communist regime in the last 100 years. When curriculum is replaced in schools, the nation is in danger. When history is erased and replaced, the nation is in danger. When teachers, professors, community leaders, and workers are removed from their jobs because of their political affiliation, the nation is danger.

Fatal paths were taken by Soviet Russia, Nazi Germany, communist China, communist Cambodia, and communist North Korea. It's an absolute travesty and dereliction of morality that America would align itself even the slightest bit with the same Marxist, socialist, and communist ideologies that have killed 100 million people over the last century. These ideologies seek to dismantle the family unit and replace it with the government. When the authority of parents to raise their children is removed by the government, the nation is in danger. When schools keep secrets from parents and undermine the authority of parents, the nation is in danger. When the government supports the "dismantling of the western nuclear family," the nation is in danger.[38] The family unit is the backbone of civilization, and any attempt to dismantle the family unit is crippling to society. Homeschooling reinforces the strength of the family unit, places parents back in the role of primary educator and as a result, strengthens society and the nation.

---

38. https://www.dailywire.com/news/black-lives-matter-what-we-believe-page-disrupt-the-western-prescribed-nuclear-family-dismantle-cisgender-privilege.

9

The Education System

At the birth of our nation, education was not promised to every citizen. Those who were able to receive an education usually did so in schools supported by churches, towns, or groups of parents, through homeschooling, or through apprenticeships. Some boarding schools were available for those who could afford the expensive tuition.[1] It's safe to say that the education system looked nothing like today's education system. The only "education system" that was in place then was to take matters into your own hands, to search for and work for your education, and to do so as local as possible — state and federal government had virtually nothing to do with education.

❧ ❧

THE DEPARTMENT OF EDUCATION

One of the earliest instances of government involvement in American education took place in 1785 and 1787 when federal ordinances were passed that granted federal lands to new

---

1. https://files.eric.ed.gov/fulltext/ED606970.pdf.

states, contingent upon their agreement to set aside a portion of those lands for public schools. Public schools became more and more popular throughout the 1800s, spreading from larger cities to more rural areas. Approximately 78% of all 5–14-year-olds were enrolled in public schools by 1870, up from 55% in 1830. In 1910, only 14% of adults over 25 had earned a high school degree, compared to 90% in 2017. Even though education was such a high priority, public education and the concept of paying for other people's kids to go to school was a hard sell.

> *In 1910, only 14% of adults over 25 had earned a high school degree, compared to 90% in 2017.*

The first Department of Education was signed into legislation and created by President Andrew Johnson in 1867.[2] Due to concerns that the Department would have too much control over education, the DOE was demoted and became the "Office" of Education just one year later. Public education continued to grow into the 20th century and so did government involvement. Federal funding for education grew in response to political and societal changes during the 1950s, 60s, and 70s. Student scores in key subject areas had improved every year for half a century, up until 1967.[3] Then in 1979, Congress passed the Department of Education Organization Act and the DOE officially began operations in 1980. Federal funding for education has continued to grow since the Department of Education was established, while at the same time America's global education ranking has declined from #3 in the 1960s to #14 in 2012.[4][5] There are two notable outcomes directly related to the government's increasing involvement in education: 1) America's educational ranking continues to drop and 2) the Bible

---

2. https://www2.ed.gov/about/overview/focus/what.html.
3. https://www.june29.com/where-did-the-us-education-system-rank-in-1979/.
4. https://www.educationnext.org/tickettonowhere/.
5. https://www.oecd.org/unitedstates/CN%20-%20United%20States.pdf.

has disappeared from schools. Government involvement has made education worse.

Do we need the DOE? The 10th Amendment to the Constitution states:

> "The powers not delegated to the United States by the Constitution, nor prohibited by it to the States, are reserved to the States respectively, or to the people."

By design, the word "education" does not appear in the U.S. Constitution, which means — according to the 10th Amendment — education should be left entirely in the hands of the states. In fact, every single state in the U.S. already has an agency or department to oversee education. Not only is the DOE unsuccessful, its existence is unconstitutional and completely unnecessary. Plain and simple, the Department of Education should not exist on the federal level.

According to the DOE website, their mission is to "promote student achievement and preparation for global competitiveness by fostering educational excellence and ensuring equal access."[6] The DOE uses grants (tax dollars) to accomplish these goals. Grants that are given out by the DOE are determined by formulas which are set by Congress. So, to receive a grant from the DOE, you'd have to meet the criteria set forth by Congress. That sounds like government influence to me.

MANDATORY STAFF TRAININGS vs. REGULAR STAFF MEETINGS

As mentioned previously, mandatory staff trainings and regular staff meetings can be used, and are being used, to push agendas and implement ideologies consistent with those of the DOE and federal government. But I want to differentiate the two

---

6. https://www2.ed.gov/about/overview/focus/what.html.

common types of meetings that teachers experience. Mandatory staff trainings and regular staff meetings are good and necessary things, when done appropriately. Teachers can grow professionally through trainings and meetings in the same way that students can grow by attending school. I take issue when staff trainings are used to usher in racist and prejudiced policies, anti-American materials, and anti-family practices.

Mandatory staff trainings are not the same as regular staff meetings. Mandatory staff trainings usually take place two or three times each school year and all teachers within the school district are required to participate. Teachers across the country participate in mandatory staff trainings each school year, as do employees in most large companies or organizations. Mandatory staff trainings for teachers are typically done online and are usually a combination of videos, slideshows, and multiple-choice questions. Teachers are required to complete trainings by a given deadline, otherwise their pay could be withheld, or they could potentially lose their job. There are usually a set of mandatory staff trainings at the beginning of the school year and at least one more set during the school year. Mandatory staff trainings usually cover topics like bloodborne pathogens, Title IX, or sexual harassment. Teachers usually complete mandatory trainings at home, on a long weekend, in between classes, and almost always when they're alone.

Mandatory trainings can be redundant and boring, but the CPS mandatory trainings I experienced during the 2020–2021 school year were very different. First, CPS began the school year remotely due to Covid, something that had never happened before. Naturally, we learned about washing our hands, wearing masks, social-distancing, and how to manage a virtual class of children. Second, the mid-year mandatory training was a complete onslaught of Critical Race Theory, Gender Theory, Marxism, socialism, and communism — which we've already covered.

Regular staff meetings are done within the school building and are usually held on a weekly basis. They are the "coffee and donuts" kind of meetings that involve a lot of laughing and joking mixed in with relevant information regarding the school, like a reading program or the upcoming school carnival. Regular staff meetings can be where school policies are created and introduced, new school programs are taught to teachers, materials are distributed, and instructions are given. School policies can even be written during regular staff meetings, either by teachers, administrators, or members of the school board.

Regular staff meetings are usually run by the building principal, but can also be run by teachers, other administrators, outside groups, agencies, or individuals. In my experience, regular staff meetings rarely, if ever, involve parents. Materials are neither screened by the community nor submitted for parental consent. The school board or Department of Education occasionally provide materials that the principal is required to present — it's usually whatever is trendy at the time. For example, the trendy phrase in 2020–2021 was "Equity." We had many regular staff meetings revolving around providing equity in school. Equity sounds great; give everyone a chance, be fair, help people. When you hear public schools talk about equity, they really mean "redistribution" — take from one group and give to another group. It's part of the socialist push in schools. The unfortunate reality is that "equity" means that schools will take resources away from students who excel academically and give them to students that underperform; in the end, both sides lose because schools will inevitably lower their standards for underperforming students to create the illusion of fairness or success.

WHERE DOES THIS TRAINING MATERIAL COME FROM?

Training materials can come from anywhere, but the progressive, CRT, and Gender Theory materials often are supplied by activist groups around the country. For example, the "Intersecting Identities" and "Gender Unicorn" graphics used in the

CPS staff trainings were from third-party groups like the California Partnership to End Domestic Violence or Trans Student Educational Resources. Other common resources would include the Department of Education, at both federal and state levels, and the school district itself. The school board is ultimately responsible, so it's critical that parents with school-aged children question their school board members about staff training materials.

Mandatory staff training materials, like what I've presented in this book, are pushed in front of teachers whether they like it or not. Materials go straight to the teachers, then to the students. Parents never see the training materials, and even if parents did eventually see the materials, the damage may already be done. If a teacher happens to have a child in the school district, then information could get passed around to the community, but that rarely seems to happen. Those teachers would be faced with the conflict I described earlier: either speak up and risk being ostracized and maybe lose your job or keep quiet and go about your business.

Mandatory staff trainings are "ground zero" for the problems I've presented in this book. As demonstrated by totalitarian regimes of the 20th century, mandatory trainings are potentially much more dangerous than the regular staff meetings, because mandatory trainings are usually completed when teachers are isolated from one another. In regular staff meetings, everyone is together. That's not to say that CRT and Gender Theory aren't permeating regular staff meetings, because they are. But mandatory staff trainings are more private, more time consuming, broader in scope, and provide no hard evidence for parents to see.

HOW DOES SCHOOL FUNDING WORK?

School funding generally works the same across the country, but there may be differences from state to state. School board members, local and state officials, and even the President of the United States are responsible for setting education policy and allocating funds. In general, public schools receive funding from local, state, and federal sources.[7] Local funding comes primarily from property taxes. State funding comes primarily from income tax and sales tax. Federal funds are distributed based on grants for special programs, usually programs that are promoted by the Department of Education, which we've already discussed. Federal funds make up almost 10% of all school funding.

Local, State, & Federal Funds
▼
Public Schools

The federal government distributes funds to states that meet certain criteria, states distribute funds to local school corporations that meet certain criteria, and local school boards distribute funds to schools that meet certain criteria. Teacher groups like the NEA and AFT can use their political influence to help set education policy, which can dictate how education funds are distributed. It represents a trickle-down system, but in reality, it's a system of schools and states jumping through symbolic, political, or ideological hoops to get more money.

Federal Funds
▼
States
▼
School Districts
▼
Schools

School boards and administrative staff are responsible for managing school budgets. Money that comes from local and state sources (property taxes, income tax, sales tax) are generally used to pay teacher salaries, utility bills for school buildings, and

---

7. https://www.publicschoolreview.com/blog/an-overview-of-the-funding-of-public-schools.

general expenses. Federal funds are used specifically for special programs — this is one way that materials for mandatory staff trainings can make their way into schools. Federal funds can have a major impact on what school's promote, even though federal funds only make up about 8–10% of school funds.

❧ ☙

FUNDING ISSUES

Government funding of public education is easily corruptible and highly wasteful. One example of this wastefulness is the disproportionate number of school administrator positions compared to teaching positions. Since 2010, the number of students and teachers in K–12 public schools has dropped, while at the same time, the number of school administrators has risen nearly 20%.

- Fall of 2010 — 49.5 million students were enrolled in public school.[8]
- Fall of 2020 — 49.4 million students were enrolled in public school.
- Fall of 2010 — 3.6 million teachers in public schools.[9]
- Fall of 2019 — 3.2 million teachers in public schools.
- 2010 — 230,000 school administrators in America.[10]
- 2021 — 274,000 school administrators in America.[11]
- 2020 — $64,133 is the average salary for a teacher.[12]
- 2021 — $102,650 is the average salary for a school administrator.[13]

---

8. https://nces.ed.gov/fastfacts/display.asp?id=372#PK12-enrollment.
9. https://nces.ed.gov/pubs2011/2011016/teachers.asp.
10. https://nces.ed.gov/pubs2012/snf201011/tables/table_03.asp?referrer=report.
11. https://www.bls.gov/oes/current/oes119032.htm.
12. https://nces.ed.gov/programs/digest/d21/tables/dt21_211.60.asp.
13. https://www.bls.gov/oes/current/oes119032.htm.

Public school administrators have little to no interaction with students, yet they earn nearly 60% more than public school teachers on average.

Below is a timeline of events during the Covid pandemic that show how the government allocated tax dollars to "support education" and the impact that teachers unions had on that process:

- Fall of 2020 — The American Academy of Pediatrics encouraged schools to fully reopen.[14]
- December 6, 2020 — The Chicago Teachers Union (CTU) tweeted, "The push to reopen schools is rooted in sexism, racism, and misogyny."
- February of 2021 — The American Federation of Teachers (AFT) and President Randi Weingarten worked with the White House and Centers for Disease Control and Prevention (CDC) on drafting Covid policy. The powerful influence of the NEA and AFT resulted in schools remaining closed.[15]
- March 11, 2021 — President Biden signed the American Rescue Plan (ARP) — a $1.9 trillion emergency package — in response to the Covid pandemic; $122 billion was directed toward public schools to address learning loss and mental health issues that occurred during the 2020–2021 school year.[16]
- Several months after CTU's tweet that wanting to reopen schools was sexist, racist, and misogynist,

14. https://nypost.com/2021/12/28/randi-weingartens-attempts-to-rewrite-school-closings-history-wont-fly/.
15. https://nypost.com/2021/05/01/teachers-union-collaborated-with-cdc-on-school-reopening-emails/.
16. https://www.whitehouse.gov/briefing-room/statements-releases/2022/03/11/fact-sheet-how-the-american-rescue-plan-is-keeping-americas-schools-open-safely-combating-learning-loss-and-addressing-student-mental-health/.

Chicago Public Schools received $525 million from the ARP's emergency Covid funds.[17]

- In response to ARP and the $122 billion emergency education funds, the NEA stated on their website, "We have an unprecedented opportunity to reshape the future of public education with the huge investment in public schools under the American Rescue Plan (ARP) Act."[18]

In summary, the largest teacher unions in the country pushed to keep schools closed, which resulted in unprecedented mental health issues and loss of learning among America's children. The federal government responded by spending $1.9 trillion on emergency relief, $122 billion of which was sent to public schools. The NEA, which is the largest labor union in the United States, having previously provided its members with Saul Alinsky's *Rules for Radicals*, after pushing to keep schools closed, and stating their desire to reshape the future of public education, now has $122 billion at their disposal. Oh, and by the way, it's on your dime. This is what government education looks like — it's a system that props itself up as the solution to all your problems, then makes everything worse. It makes the decisions on behalf of the parents, tells the students what to believe, and punishes and isolates those that would dare to step out of line. This is the way of a lost and corrupt system, but it doesn't have to be this way for your family. The choice to homeschool can remove the politics and corruption of the federal government, the DOE, school boards, and teacher unions from interfering with your child's education.

---

17. https://www.cps.edu/strategic-initiatives/moving-forward-together/).
18. https://www.nea.org/advocating-for-change/covid/funding-the-recovery.

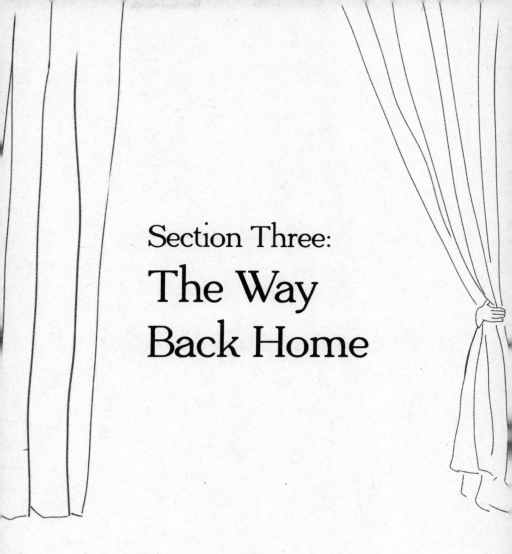

Section Three:
The Way Back Home

"Thus saith the LORD, stand ye in the ways, and see, and ask for the old paths, where is the good way, and walk therein, and ye shall find rest for your souls."
— Jeremiah 6:16

10

Parents Matter

We learn in the Bible, through common sense, and by hard data that godly parents make all the difference in the world. There is an intentional, systematic, and devastating war that's being waged on parents and traditional family values in this country. It's not just a difference of ideals or a matter of education — it's a spiritual battle over the souls of children. Parents, particularly Christian parents who are married, are the first model of the Gospel that their children will learn — even before learning to read, write, or tie their own shoes. Christian morals will not be reinforced in public schools, in fact, they will be challenged and persecuted, and parents, once again, will be undermined. Homeschooling is a way that God can be brought back into the home, back into education, and back into the hearts and minds of children.

We learn from Ephesians 6:1–4 the proper dynamic between parents and children.

"Children, obey your parents in the Lord: for this is right. Honor thy father and mother." By being taught to obey their parents, children are prepared to understand that Jesus was always obedient to His Heavenly Father.

"Fathers, provoke not your children to wrath: but bring them up in the nurture and admonition of the Lord." Being godly parents actually models the characteristics of God for your children. By having parents that love them, children are prepared to understand that God loves them, too.

Children can observe and understand God's design and His salvation model, simply by having parents that live according to God's Word. Once a child reaches the point where they are able to comprehend the Gospel, it will make sense to them because they will have seen it modeled by their parents their whole life. That child, as a result, will be more prepared to receive the Gospel message. But if this process and biblical preparation can be cut off and stopped, if parents can be undermined, and if the child's mind can be captured by indoctrination at an early age, then how will that child respond when they hear a Gospel they're taught is oppressive, coming from a Bible they're taught is abusive? Atheist ideologies, found in many public schools around the country, are being used to attack the family institution, which was established by God.

BLM AND DISRUPTING THE WESTERN NUCLEAR FAMILY

One of the most prominent cultural movements permeating schools in America today is the Black Lives Matter movement, which was founded by self-described trained Marxists. Karl Marx, also known as the "Father of Communism" once stated, "My life's object is to dethrone God and destroy capitalism."[1] BLM posters and slogans are commonplace in mandatory staff trainings, and in classrooms and school hallways all over the country. BLM provides programs to schools which promote their agendas to K–12 students. BLM's "What We Believe"

---

1. http://libertytree.ca/quotes/Karl.Marx.Quote.EBAB.

page once stated, "We disrupt the Western-prescribed nuclear family."[2] After receiving much criticism about their beliefs, BLM removed the page altogether. Why would anyone want to disrupt a family unit of father, mother, and children? Let's talk about what happens when the "western-prescribed nuclear family" is disrupted.

Approximately 40% of children in America are born to single mothers and 25% of all children live without a biological, step, or adoptive father in the home.[3] Studies show that nearly 60% of all fatherless homes in the United States come from the black community, even though the black community makes up approximately 13% of the general population.[4] Why would a group like BLM, that claims to care about black lives, promote an ideology that has a disproportionately negative effect on the black population? Isn't that the opposite of what they claim to be trying to do? That is an outright attack, not just on black families, but on all families!

The United States Department of Justice and National Public Radio provide the following statistics[5] on children who come from fatherless homes:

- 2x more likely to suffer from obesity
- 2x more likely to drop out of high school
- 2x more likely to commit suicide
- 3x more likely to go to prison (85% of the current youth prison population came from fatherless homes)
- 3x more likely to sell drugs or carry a gun for offensive purposes
- 4x more likely to live in poverty

2. https://www.dailywire.com/news/black-lives-matter-what-we-be-lieve-page-disrupt-the-western-prescribed-nuclear-family-dismantle-cisgen-der-privilege.
3. https://www.fatherhood.org/father-absence-statistic.
4. https://lifeisbeautiful.org/statistics-on-fatherless-homes/#:~:text=%28Na-tional%20Public%20Radio%29%20%237.%2057%25%20of%20the%20fatherless,have%20a%2020%25%20fatherless%20rate.%20%28National%20Public%20Radio%29.
5. https://www.fatherhood.org/father-absence-statistic.

- 7x more likely to become pregnant as a teen
- Increased likelihood of behavior issues
- Increased likelihood of substance abuse
- More likely to run away from home and become homeless

Since the school shooting at Columbine High School in 1999, approximately 75% of school shooters have come from broken households — not just of divorce, but child abuse, domestic violence, substance abuse, and crime.[6] Without a doubt, the importance of a strong nuclear family cannot be overstated. Children need a strong family, they need morals, they need parents, they need a mom and a dad at home together. BLM claims to be advocating for black lives, but their Marxist beliefs actually weaken families and communities. The negative consequences of fatherless homes show just how important and valuable the nuclear family is. Children need parents and, statistically, children with both a mother and a father at home are much better off. Schools should not be promoting BLM as some sort of champion for equality.

> *Since the school shooting at Columbine High School in 1999, approximately 75% of school shooters have come from broken households — not just of divorce, but child abuse, domestic violence, substance abuse, and crime.*

⟋⟍ ⟍⟋

GROOMING

Grooming is a new and disturbing trend that takes place all over the country, including in public schools where students are indoctrinated with extreme versions of Gender Theory, taught by teachers and staff who engage in the sexualization of students as young as kindergarten. Graphics such as the

6. https://www.heritage.org/marriage-and-family/commentary/the-crisis-fatherless-shooters.

"Gender Unicorn" and "Genderbread Man" are two examples of how impressionable elementary students are being exposed to homosexual and transgender ideologies. These characters are presented to students as adorable, fun, and friendly characters — what kid wouldn't want to be just like them?! This is just the beginning of the grooming process as students are later being recruited by teachers (often in secret) in middle school and high school to join groups such as the Gay Straight Alliance and other LGBTQ clubs. As in Illinois and California, public school staff members are not obligated to notify parents if their child identifies as gay, trans, non-binary, or even uses a different name entirely. In fact, these teachers are forbidden by state law to notify parents of such occurrences. This is a form of kidnapping and child abuse which is being sponsored by the state, all on the taxpayer's dime.

One example of grooming in public schools comes from Buena Vista Middle School in California. During the 2020–2021 school year, two middle school teachers worked together to create a secret pro-LGBTQ club for students. The teachers stated in a California Teachers Association meeting that they would regularly monitor student google searches, note their internet activity, and listen to private conversations between students to identify prospective club members. Once a student was identified, the teachers would give that student a personal invitation to join their club. To hide the club from parents, the two teachers changed the name of the club from the Gay-Straight Alliance (GSA) to "The Equity Club."[7] This was an unofficial club, so student attendance was not recorded and there was no roster. This was an intentional move by the teachers because it gave them deniability in case a parent asked

---

7. https://www.dailywire.com/news/shock-report-ca-teachers-urge-recruiting-kids-into-lgbt-clubs?utm_term=&utm_campaign=dw_conversions_sub-scriptions_performancemax_na&utm_source=adwords&utm_medi-um=ppc&hsa_acc=6411461344&hsa_cam=16590646933&hsa_grp=&h-sa_ad=&hsa_src=x&hsa_tgt=&hsa_kw=&hsa_mt=&hsa_net=adwords&h-sa_ver=3&gclid=CjwKCAjw-8qVBhANEiwAfjXLrszlcDIAH8SMwK-CfM4YYnXtuYGL24o2a1i95-4rr26d3Lj-rb9RRxRoChhsQAvD_BwE.

about their child joining the club. The teachers would respond to any parental inquiry by saying that they didn't know if a student signed in or attended a club meeting, because there was no roster kept. One of the teachers stated, "We would never want a kid to get in trouble for attending if their parents are upset." The teachers even devised a plan outlining precisely when they would teach students about gender — it would be done at a certain time of year with the sole intention of denying parents the opportunity to object to their teachings.

In 2021, staff at this school notified one set of parents that their 12-year-old daughter was now a boy; a transition that had taken place at their school, without parental knowledge or consent. The teachers allegedly changed the girl's name, referred to the girl with male pronouns, and changed her school accounts to align with the new identity without the parents having any knowledge.[8] The parents refused to refer to their daughter as a boy and a public safety officer was called into the meeting to urge the parents to use the "preferred" pronouns. It's as if the school said, "Sorry parents, we've taken your child's mind and completely warped it. You no longer have a daughter; you have a 'son.' We've deemed ourselves worthy and qualified to sexualize your child and they belong to us now. You must now follow our trans rules or face the consequences."

The sexual assault on children is even promoted on the federal level. In July of 2022, the Assistant Secretary for Health, Rachel Levine (a biological man that identifies as a woman) spoke out in support of medical procedures for children to affirm their gender identity. Levine said, "We really want to base our treatment and to affirm and to support and empower these youths not to limit their participation in activities in sports and even limit their ability to get gender affirmation treatment in their state."[9] "Gender affirmation treatment"

8. https://www.dailywire.com/news/resign-or-repent-watch-as-parents-unload-on-teachers-they-say-secretly-coached-12-year-old-daughter-into-being-trans.

9. https://www.foxnews.com/media/rachel-levine-blasted-call-support-empower-youth-transgender-treatments-unserious-regime.

includes transition surgeries and puberty blockers. These are procedures that would have devastating effects and would cause irreversible damage on children across the country, not just physically, but mentally and emotionally as well. It is not the role of schools or the state to affirm a child's gender identification, especially to the point of physical mutilation (i.e., "top surgeries"). It's the role of schools to teach children reading, writing, and arithmetic —

> *It is not the role of schools or the state to affirm a child's gender identification, especially to the point of physical mutilation (i.e., "top surgeries"). It's the role of schools to teach children reading, writing, and arithmetic — not Gender Theory and sex-change operations.*

not Gender Theory and sex-change operations. These people are coming for your children, even at high levels of the U.S. government.

The federal government is now funding the implementation of Gender Theory and the LGBTQ ideology in K-12 schools. In 2022, the CDC began offering a new grant program which would provide K-12 schools with up to $350k, contingent upon the school promoting LGBTQ ideology. Schools that receive this grant must first meet certain requirements including 1) forming a Gender and Sexuality Alliance or Gay-Straight Alliance (GSA) group for students, and 2) requiring school staff to receive annual training on how to support LGBTQ students and implement "inclusive curricula." The so-called "inclusive curricula," of course, excludes any beliefs or opinions that differ from even the most far-left LGBTQ ideology. The CDC website provides resources for K-12 schools to help them achieve these requirements; one such resource is titled, *"Schools in Transition: A Guide for Supporting Transgender Students in K-12 Schools."* [10] This guide was created through the collaborative efforts of the ACLU, a group

10. https://www.cdc.gov/healthyyouth/safe-supportive-environments/PD-LGBTQ.htm

called Gender Spectrum, the Human Rights Campaign, the National Center for Lesbian Rights, and the National Education Association. Its guiding principles state that it is "healthy, appropriate, and typical" for K-12 students to express a transgender identity. Further, it states that parents "must continue to expand their understanding" of gender ideology and that students should be referred to by their preferred pronouns, even if outside of male or female pronouns.[11] Thus, if parents do not support their child's transgender identity (for whatever reason, including a genuine belief that the child is not actually transgender), the solution is just to "expand your understanding" —problem solved.

This CDC resource also states that students (or parents) that express concern about sharing a locker room or restroom with a transgender student are simply operating "based on the false idea that a transgender boy is not a 'real' boy, and a transgender girl is not a 'real' girl." The United States federal government (the CDC is a federal agency) believes it's a "false idea" and "misconception" to consider a biological boy to be a boy and a biological girl to be a girl. This antiscientific delusion is being pushed into K-12 schools all over our country and is being propped up by our federal government with our tax dollars.

In response to "unsupportive parents," the transition guide states that "the school and student should determine how to proceed through the collaborative process of figuring out how the school can support the student and balance the student's need to be affirmed at school with the reality that the student does not have that support at home." Read that again — the *school* is now going to meet the "needs" of the student. According to them, children "need" to be told repeatedly that they're not who the really are and that being transgender is "healthy, appropriate, and typical." Regardless of any proof that the child genuinely has gender dysphoria or problems at home, or even

---

11. https://hrc-prod-requests.s3-us-west-2.amazonaws.com/files/assets/resources-In-Transition.pdf

basic communication with parents, the school can take over the parental role simply because a child says his or her parents don't approve. I don't know about you, but when I was a child, my parents didn't approve of me doing a lot of things—drinking, smoking, cussing—and that's what parents are supposed to do. Children need parental guidance in all aspects of life, but especially ones as fundamental as identity.

"Foolishness is bound in the heart of a child, but the rod of correction shall drive it far from him" — Proverbs 22:15.

The Word of God teaches that it is loving to correct and discipline a child and that it is not loving to leave them to their own devices to fend for themselves.

"He who spares his rod hates his son, but he who loves him disciplines him promptly." — Proverbs 13:24

To be fair, schools (rightly) have policies in place that are meant to protect students from physically abusive parents — if a student comes to school with bruises, cuts, or physical injuries — but it must be documented and tracked over time. However, there is a great contrast when it comes to children being transgender — all it takes for a school to push parents out is for a student to accuse their parents of not accepting them. So, once the parents are removed from the equation, the children are given over to their teachers and school staff, who have control of the children for eight hours a day, five days a week. Teachers, like the thousands I worked with in Chicago Public Schools and the ones that receive grant money from the CDC, are trained to reinforce and support the transgender "identity" of these young, impressionable children by constantly praising them for identifying as transgender. These kids don't stand a chance!

"Before I formed thee in the belly I knew thee."
— Jeremiah 1:5

Additionally, schools are instructed to educate parents on the needs of the child, as opposed to the parents educating the schools about their own child—this is the opposite of how it should be. Standard procedure is for schools to recommend mental health or medical providers, support groups, and therapists to help promote family acceptance. The default position is that the professionals know what's best for students and that it's always best to affirm the child's feelings as opposed to teaching the child objective, biological truth. This unrelenting dedication to affirm a child's transgender identity extends to the point of medical transitions including the use of hormone blockers, which they claim, "act as a pause button and give the youth an opportunity to explore their gender identity without the distress of developing the permanent, unwanted physical characteristics of their assigned sex at birth." This claim is unfounded and not supported by medical research — not to mention in direct opposition to biblical teaching. This is an extremely dangerous slippery slope that children are being pushed closer and closer to in K-12 schools.

Another resource provided by the CDC is the Gay-Straight Alliance Network, which guides schools, staff, and students on various LGBTQ related topics, such as "Dealing with Hostility and Opposition."[12] To combat the issues of "hostility and oppression," the GSA Network recommends that GSA clubs in K-12 schools hold secret meetings in secret locations, and that secret invitations should be given to select students by adult staff members who support and affirm LGBTQ students, in secret of course. This is a well-documented strategy that's being recommended by the CDC and may be implemented by over 4,000 GSA clubs in K-12 schools around the country.[13] To reiterate, the strategy is to hold secret meetings, in secret locations, facilitated by adults that hand-pick students to be indoctrinated with inherently sexual content and no parental knowledge or approval. What could go wrong?! Why are five-year-olds going to school and coming home discussing transgenderism? Why are adult men and women secretly inviting children to secret meetings in secret locations and discussing sex? And why is the Center for Disease Control and Prevention — of all agencies — superintending all of this? This national obsession over sexualizing children — which is evil and predatory — is becoming more and more prevalent in schools, which should be the safest environment outside of home and church.

To summarize, the federal government is directing tax dollars to the CDC. The CDC then gives that money to schools, via grants, but only if those schools establish GSA clubs and implement what the CDC refers to as "inclusive curricula" intended to expose (at best) or indoctrinate (at worst) young children with their values on sex, sexuality, and gender identity — without parental knowledge or consent, let alone presenting any contrary opinion.

There is a clear, concerted, intentional effort to indoctrinate and sexualize young children and promote homosexuality over heterosexuality regardless of children's actual sexual

12. https://gsanetwork.org/resources/dealing-with-hostility-opposition/
13. https://www.upward.news/cdc-to-use-85-million-to-pressure-schools-adopt-lgbt/

orientation (or before children even know what that term means). Children are the target here, not mature adults. This trend is alarming and disturbing. If adults were to discuss sexuality at the workplace or suggest a coworker transition to another gender, that may very well be considered sexual harassment. But if teachers talk to elementary students about the same subject, it's supposed to be acceptable?! Absolutely not! Jesus gave perhaps His harshest teaching on the subject of causing children to sin or harming children. He said, "Whoever causes one of these little ones who believe in Me to sin, it would be better for him if a millstone were hung around his neck, and he were drowned in the depth of the sea." — Matthew 18:6; NKJV. This is a dire warning not just to teachers and schools, but to our nation as a whole. Our children must be protected, nurtured, and raised in the ways of the Lord. We must take a stand against this immoral and predatory conduct, otherwise we can expect to see more instances of children being manipulated, sexualized, and victimized in schools.

UNDERMINING THE ROLE OF PARENTS

Public schools are systematically separating parents from their child's education process. Educators at the highest level are advocating for parents having limited influence over what their children are taught in school. The average student is in school seven hours a day, 180 days a year, for 13 years straight. If parents don't fill the role of primary educator at home, then schools will fill that role in the classroom. The right of parents to teach values to their children is being undermined by the public school system. Parental influence is removed and leaves a void that's being filled with Gender Theory, Critical Race Theory, and Marxist/communist propaganda.

A Virginia delegate is working to draft a new bill that would criminally prosecute parents for not affirming their transgender child.[14] Virginia Delegate Elizabeth Guzman initially drafted a bill in 2020 that redefined the term "abused or neglected child" to include children who have a "mental injury on the basis of the child's gender identity or sexual orientation." The initial bill did not pass committee; the only Senate support came from Virginia Senator Joe Morrissey, who served prison time after being indicted on possession of child pornography. Child Protective Services already has the power to remove abused children from abusive homes and place them in foster care and thank goodness for that. However, this bill classifies it as "mental abuse" if a parent does not affirm his or her child's transgender identity (for any reason). By connecting "mental abuse" with physical abuse, this bill would pave the way for children being taken from their "abusive" parents just because the parents disagree on transgenderism. The proposed bill would further empower teachers and social workers to report parents to Child Protective Services and possibly charge the parents with a felony or misdemeanor for such "mental abuse." It is difficult to read this any way other than an attempt to blackmail parents with custody of their children — or even employment —by stating that a "CPS charge could harm your employment ... because nowadays many people do a CPS database search before offering employment." So, either you offer your child upon the altar of transgenderism, or you may never work or see your child again.

Parents are the largest stakeholders in the education of their children and should have the most say in the process. For example, if you are the largest shareholder for Google, then you'll have the most influence over that company. You should have the right to voice your approval or disapproval

Parents are the largest stakeholders in the education of their children and should have the most say in the process.

14. https://www.dailywire.com/news/virginia-democrat-bill-would-criminal-ly-prosecute-parents-who-dont-affirm-their-kids-as-transgender.

of how the company functions. Parents should have the same rights over their children in schools without the threat of being labeled as a domestic threat.

How much control should parents have over curriculum? What is a realistic expectation? A teacher cannot poll dozens, even hundreds of parents each school year to gather their list of approved ideas for the curriculum — that's ridiculous. Parents cannot give up their livelihoods to be in classrooms every day, making decisions on instruction — that's unrealistic. Then again, parents cannot hand their children over to be raised by the public school system — that would be irresponsible. Teachers cannot be robots that show no independent thought or human emotion — they should be able to model values and behaviors for their students. There is a conflict between parental involvement and what's actually feasible in the long-term. There is another conflict between schools undermining the role of parents and teachers being left alone to do their jobs.

If the parents don't make decisions for their children, public schools will. On October 21, 2021, the Washington Post published an article titled "Parents claim they have the right to shape their kids' school curriculum. They don't." The article, written by Jack Schneider and Jennifer Berkshire, implies that parents are radicals if they seek to influence their child's curriculum, and that turning over decisions to parents would limit a child's ability to think independently.[15] According to this article, when parents push to have rights over their child's education, it's cast aside as purely a political move. But, when the state pushes to have sole rights to a child's education, it's portrayed as being for the well-being of the child — this is bizzarro world! The article further states that by instilling ideas and values in their children, parents are impeding their children from learning *other* ideas and values (by now it's pretty clear what the *other* ideas and values are). It seems

---

15. https://www.washingtonpost.com/outlook/parents-rights-protests-kids/2021/10/21/5cf4920a-31d4-11ec-9241-aad8e48f01ff_story.html.

that groups such as the AFT and NEA want the kids all to themselves without having to compete with those pesky parents. The article states that children should learn to think for themselves, thus creating a necessary separation of child and parent; parents just seem to always be in the way.

Randi Weingarten is the President of the American Federation of Teachers (AFT), a group that represents over 1.7 million teachers and is the second largest teacher group in the country.[16] In a tweet on October 25, 2021, Weingarten praised this article that claimed parents do not have the right to shape curriculum. Weingarten posted the article on her personal Twitter account, voicing her support by saying, "Great piece on parents' rights and #publicschools."[17]

This article casts parents as radicals that are hurting their children by controlling what values they learn. The answer, apparently, is to give over control to the government system and let the professionals teach your children morality. These are ideals embraced by Randi Weingarten, the AFT, and millions of teachers across the country. Schools are encouraging children to break from their parents under the guise of "thinking for themselves," when schools want to push their own agenda on them. The public school agenda consists of policies, textbooks, curriculum, and initiatives that are entirely one-sided, endorsing only progressive/leftist ideologies. Public schools don't teach children *how* to think, they teach children *what* to think.

Public schools don't teach children how to think, they teach children what to think.

Parents pay taxes so their children can go to public schools eight hours a day, five days a week, 180 days a year — they deserve to know what's going on. We can shop for regular things like food, clothes, cars, and houses, and if we don't like any of it we can buy something else; public schools don't allow that option. We have endless options for rather meaningless

16. https://www.aft.org/about.
17. https://twitter.com/rweingarten.

things, but when it comes to educating our children, it's one-size-fits-all. Sure, parents can pay exorbitant amounts on tuition for private schools, but their tax dollars will still go to the public schools. It makes sense that parents should be able to screen *everything* before it's given to their children and have influence if they don't like it.

⸎ ⸎

SCHOOL SHOOTINGS

The importance of the nuclear family — mother, father, children — cannot be overstated. For example, three of the most infamous school shooters came from broken homes.

- Sandy Hook Elementary School — the school shooter's father had not seen his son in over two years and was quoted as saying he wished his son "had never been born."[18]

- Stoneman Douglas High School — the school shooter was adopted as a newborn; the adoptive father died when the school shooter was a young child; the biological mother had an extensive criminal record and biological father was not involved in his life.

- Buell Elementary School — the youngest school shooter in America's history was six years old; his father was in jail at the time of the shooting.

Certainly, not every broken home yields such tragic results, but you can't help but wonder how things may have been different for these children had their nuclear families been more stable.

How did school shootings become so normalized? A short answer is the collective turning away from God as a nation,

---

18. https://www.heritage.org/marriage-and-family/commentary/the-crisis-fatherless-shooters.

moral decay, devaluing of the sanctity of life, and the breaking down of the family unit. The tragic and chaotic consequences of America's rejection of God are playing out in real-time, right before our eyes; the regularity and normality of school shootings is perhaps the clearest indication that our nation has lost its way. In the last ten years (2013–2022) there were 943 incidences of gunfire on school grounds, resulting in 321 deaths and 652 injuries.[19]

Mass shootings and school shootings date back to the time of America's birth; it's not a new phenomenon. However, what is of great concern is the fact that 20 out of the 27 deadliest mass shootings in America's history have taken place since 2007.[20] The last two and a half decades have simultaneously been the worst era for school shootings and mass shootings in America. Guns, mental illness, political division, and racism have always existed in America — to varying degrees. But for over 220 years, we didn't have this level of school shootings and mass shootings. So, what's changed? What's causing this spike?

We can learn from history as time passes and recognize certain trends or outliers over time. Certain things do stand out culturally as being relatively new compared to the previous 220 years; a few examples are:

- The legal restriction of Bibles being given to students in schools is relatively new.
- The record-high number of fatherless homes is relatively new.
- The internet is relatively new.
- Social media is relatively new.
- Video games are relatively new.
- The overall decline in morality is relatively new.
- The high rate of depression among teenagers is relatively new.

19. https://everytownresearch.org/maps/gunfire-on-school-grounds/.
20. https://www.dailywire.com/news/walsh-mass-shootings-matt-walsh.

- The all-time low number of Americans believing in God is relatively new.[21]
- The record number of children and adults on prescription drugs is relatively new.

The laundry list goes on and on because a broken system can't fix itself. So how can we fix these problems? The short answer is a return to God, morals, and family.

"If My people who are called by My name will humble themselves, and pray and seek My face, and turn from their wicked ways, then I will hear from heaven, and will forgive their sin and heal their land." — 2 Chronicles 7:14; NKJV

ACTIVE SHOOTER DRILLS IN SCHOOL

What exactly constitutes a school shooting? According to the Center for Homeland Defense and Security, there really isn't a clear definition. For example, if a student brandishes a gun at school but is stopped before firing the weapon — that incident would be included in the K–12 School Shooting Database.[22] If a school officer's gun is accidentally discharged — that could also be entered in the national database. Both examples are dangerous, of course, but not quite in the same category as the school shootings that result in the death of students and teachers. There are multiple government agencies that collect a variety of data related to school shootings or school violence; sometimes data is shared between datasets and sometimes it's not. For example, a violent incident at school that does not involve a firearm may still be entered into the same dataset as a school shooting. Also, a shooting involving students but occurring off school grounds may still be considered a school

---

21. https://news.gallup.com/poll/393737/belief-god-dips-new-low.aspx.
22. https://www.chds.us/ssdb/methods/#defining.

shooting. School shooting data also includes incidences that occur at preschools, colleges, vocational schools, and technical institutions — not just K–12 schools. The definition is vague and casts a wide net to gather as much research as possible to prevent such incidents from happening in the future. With all of that in mind, at least one thing is clear — the number of students and teachers that have been shot and killed in American public schools in the last 30 years is an ongoing national tragedy. Sadly, for students, preparing for a school shooter has become part of the regular school experience, like a fire drill.

Sadly, for students, preparing for a school shooter has become part of the regular school experience, like a fire drill.

It's common for schools across the country to have Emergency Action Plans (EAP). Emergency procedures are not exclusive to public and private schools. Homeschool families can have emergency procedures at home, too; many families do and rightfully so. An EAP establishes protocols and procedures for a variety of emergencies, such as what to do if there is a robbery in the area, a car chase, a stranger in the building, or an active shooter in the building. Schools practice these safety procedures on a regular basis — maybe once a month, once a quarter, once a semester, or once a year. Teachers are trained first, and then teachers can practice with their students as often as they'd like. The Department of Homeland Security defines an "active shooter" as "an individual actively engaged in killing or attempting to kill people in a confined and populated area; in most cases, active shooters use firearms and there is no pattern or method to their selection of victims."[23] Many active shooter situations are over (ex: suicide) before law enforcement can be on the scene, which means innocent bystanders (teachers, students) are completely defenseless and must resort to hiding and locking the classroom door. In the case

23. https://www.dhs.gov/xlibrary/assets/active_shooter_booklet.pdf.

of the Uvalde, Texas, school shooting in 2022, officers did not engage the active shooter for over one hour (77 minutes) after the first shots were fired in the building.[24] It's absolutely horrifying and infuriating to think about.

When I was teaching in Indiana as an Elementary P.E. Teacher, my school would hold one staff meeting at the beginning of the school year that was dedicated to our EAP and what to do in case of an active shooter. Several members of the local police department would lead the meeting, give instructions, and answer questions. Our active shooter procedure had a different name that changed over time — it was either "Code Red" or "Lockdown." I taught in a gymnasium for most of my career, so my active shooter/lockdown procedures were a little different compared to those of classroom teachers. Since students were not as familiar with the gym as they were with their regular classrooms, I made it a point to practice our lockdowns as soon as the school year started. This is an awkward situation for anyone to be in, because you have to gently explain the importance of practicing these procedures and why we're practicing them without scaring a five-year-old or kindergartner. In the world today, it's a necessary evil.

In such a procedure, our principal would make an announcement over the intercom, I would lock the outer doors right away and quickly usher my students into our designated hiding spot. Once there, I would instruct the students to sit down against the wall and be as quiet as possible. Then, I'd turn the lights off. Students would then sit in complete darkness, shoulder to shoulder, and struggling with trying not to giggle while simultaneously being afraid that this is actually a real, life-threatening situation. Some kids would get scared and cry, which would scare other kids and make them cry. On occasion, this would turn into a shushing battle between the students and me, in which case I would have to use my teacher voice to

---

24. https://www.texastribune.org/2022/06/20/uvalde-police-shooting-response-records/.

regain control — not a good situation. We were to remain there until a police officer unlocked our door to let us out. Otherwise, we had to stay put, in the dark, for as long as it took.

The reason I shared these emergency procedures is to ask parents:

> Who would you rather have guiding your children through this process — you, or the public school system?

> Who would you rather have help your kids process and understand what these things mean — you, or the public school system?

> Are you comfortable with the public school system influencing and shaping your children in sensitive situations for up to eight hours a day?

After all, this is the same system that is sexualizing children, teaching Gender Theory, enabling the transgender craze, pushing Critical Race Theory, has school boards calling parents "domestic terrorists," outlaws the Bible, says boys can be girls and girls can be boys, and is plagued with the fear of perpetual school shooters.

Has the culture of school shootings become so common in our society that we don't think twice about sending our five-year-old children off to potential warzones where they practice what to do if a shooter comes into their classroom? Public education is completely out of control. This is a broken system that is crippling students and destroying families.

11

The Benefits
of Homeschooling

Homeschooling can be the solution to the public school problem. It's okay for homeschooling to look different from public school — it supposed to be different, in fact it's good to be different. It's okay if you finish your school day before lunch and take regular breaks to go on walks or play. Plus, homeschooling is welcoming to people of every race, income level, political leaning, and faith, unlike the public school doctrine of "Intersecting Identities". The most valuable thing that homeschooling can offer families is the opportunity to build relationships with each other and with God. Other benefits include:

- Better academic performance! Homeschoolers typically score 15–30 percentile points higher than public school students on standardized tests.
- Saving money! It costs taxpayers an average of $15,240 a year to educate one public school student. For the average American family, it only

costs $600 to educate a homeschool student for a year.[1]

- Freedom to create a schedule that works for your family.
- Freedom to choose a curriculum you want.
- Parents are reinstated as the primary educator.
- Instilling desired morals and values into all aspects of education.
- Families can escape the unnecessary and often harmful pressures that come with public and private schools.
- Homeschool students perform significantly better statistically on social, emotional, and psychological development than those in conventional schools.
- Adults who were home educated succeed and perform significantly better statistically than those who attended institutional schools.
- Homeschoolers participate in community service more, vote more, attend public meetings more, and succeed at college more frequently than the general population.
- Children are protected from being sexualized through "Gender Unicorns," the "Gender-bread Man," drag-queen story hours, and forced LGBTQ celebrations.
- Children are protected from school bullying.
- Parents know their children better than anyone else and love their children more than anyone else.

Homeschooling bests public schooling in virtually every metric and there is no solid evidence that homeschooling has any negative impact on students compared to public schooling. For families on the fence about homeschool vs. public school — the case is closed on the benefits of homeschooling.

---

1. https://www.nheri.org/research-facts-on-homeschooling/.

Homeschooling bests public schooling in virtually every metric and there is no solid evidence that homeschooling has any negative impact on students compared to public schooling.

Some private schools can provide an escape from the indoctrination that's taking place in public schools. Unfortunately, not all private schools are created equal, and many have adopted the same woke curriculum as public schools. However, families that are unsatisfied with the direction or performance of their private school can take their money elsewhere. As a result, private schools tend to bend to the will of parents a little more than public schools. Currently, private school families pay tuition on top of their local taxes which support the public school — even though they're not using the public schools.

Public school has been the norm for families for nearly a hundred years. Citizens pay taxes and part of those taxes go toward a free public education for children. As schools have grown more and more political over time, biblical values have been removed and wokeness has taken over. Now, parents are stuck paying the bill for their kids to be indoctrinated with CRT and Gender Theory, whether they like it or not.

THE SCHOOL CHOICE MOVEMENT

The School Choice movement deserves some attention as it has become increasingly popular in conservative states, with lawmakers, and with families who are looking for public school alternatives. School choice endorses the use of tax credits, vouchers, and educational savings accounts families can use to send their children to a school of their choice, whether it be a public school, private school, charter school, homeschool, or online learning.[2] This would allow homeschool families to use

2. https://www.federationforchildren.org/school-choice-america/.

their tax dollars to educate their own children as opposed to funding public school systems; this is what's known as "funding students, not systems."

While school choice may sound like a positive solution to the public school monopoly on education, there are potentially dangerous strings attached. The problem is, tax dollars are still tax dollars, no matter how they're used. This means that families who use tax dollars (tax credits, vouchers...) to homeschool their children, would eventually become subject to government oversight, which is the whole problem with education in the first place. The results could be that only certain curricula are approved, parents may be subject to mandatory trainings (just like the trainings I experienced in Chicago Public Schools), and family homes may be subject to government audits. In essence, charter schools, private schools, and homeschools could simply become another form of government-run schools — no different from the public schools that we have right now. Families could be backed into a corner with no way out. "Funding students, not systems" may sound great and be well-meaning, but the outcome could be devastating.

❦

WHAT IF YOU CAN'T HOMESCHOOL?

The case for homeschooling is extremely compelling, but there are many families that — for a variety of reasons — will continue to send their children to public or private schools. For those families I offer the following suggestions (as mentioned in chapter 1) based on my teaching experiences:

- Talk to your children daily about what they're learning at school.
- Demand that you be involved in your school's textbook and curriculum adoption process.

- Demand opportunities to join your school's regular grade level meetings and department meetings.
- Demand access to all mandatory staff trainings; the same training that the teachers complete.
- Demand cameras be installed in every classroom.
- Participate in local elections (school board, sheriff, mayor, state representatives, etc.).
- Run for school board member positions yourself.
- Push to have elected school boards instead of appointed school boards.
- Attend school board meetings regularly and schedule time to speak and ask questions.
- Communicate with teachers and principals on a regular basis.
- Join the PTO and attend meetings.
- Monitor daily assignments, field trip details, school speakers, and special school assemblies.

In short — it's best to be involved and to be proactive. Parents can't always count on teachers, principals, or the PTO to make the right decisions; it's up to the parents. Speaking to your children, their teachers, and their administrators on a daily basis, showing up to meetings, asking hard questions, joining school groups, and forming parent-teacher groups are great ways to prevent the indoctrination process and to prevent the public school system from systematically driving a wedge between you and children.

"What shall it profit a man, if he shall gain the whole world, and lose his own soul?" — Mark 8:36. Nothing, as a parent, is more important than the soul of your children. Every family is unique and has their own set of unique challenges, but all parents are tasked with training up their children in the way they should go. Educating children is difficult but it's an investment worth making and one that can pay eternal dividends.

Additional Homeschool Resources

Answers for Homeschooling
You've made the decision to homeschool. Suddenly, you find that some of those who were once in your corner supporting you are now questioning your competency as a parent and maybe even your sanity. This book equips you to answer the critic in your life with resolve and confidence.

Education: Does God Have an Opinion?
A Scriptural guide designed to help you disciple and educate your children in agreement with God's Word. Many Christians believe God doesn't care about how children are schooled or the methods of education that are employed. This book uses the Bible to prove otherwise.

IndoctriNation
Exposes the government's agenda as being far less than neutral regarding Christianity. Learn the history and philosophy of America's public school education and discover the anti-biblical brainwashing happening there. Reveals the anti-Christian ideologies at work in today's classroom, including humanism, Marxism, and more.